Predictive Analytics with SAS and R

Ramchandra S Mangrulkar •
Pallavi Vijay Chavan

Predictive Analytics with SAS and R

Core Concepts, Tools, and Implementation

Apress®

Ramchandra S Mangrulkar
Computer Engineering
D. J. Sanghvi
Mumbai, Maharashtra, India

Pallavi Vijay Chavan
Flat No. C1004, Near Ganesh Temple
Exotica, Casa Rio
Mumbai, Maharashtra, India

ISBN-13 (pbk): 979-8-8688-0904-0   ISBN-13 (electronic): 979-8-8688-0905-7
https://doi.org/10.1007/979-8-8688-0905-7

Managing Director, Apress Media LLC: Welmoed Spahr
Acquisitions Editor: Smriti Srivastava
Development Editor: Laura Berendson
Coordinating Editor: Kripa Joseph

Cover designed by eStudioCalamar

Cover image designed by Unsplash

Distributed to the book trade worldwide by Springer Science+Business Media New York, 1 New York Plaza, Suite 4600, New York, NY 10004-1562, USA. Phone 1-800-SPRINGER, fax (201) 348-4505, e-mail orders-ny@springer-sbm.com, or visit www.springeronline.com. Apress Media, LLC is a California LLC and the sole member (owner) is Springer Science + Business Media Finance Inc (SSBM Finance Inc). SSBM Finance Inc is a **Delaware** corporation.
For information on translations, please e-mail booktranslations@springernature.com; for reprint, paperback, or audio rights, please e-mail bookpermissions@springernature.com
Apress titles may be purchased in bulk for academic, corporate, or promotional use. eBook versions and licenses are also available for most titles. For more information, reference our Print and eBook Bulk Sales web page at http://www.apress.com/bulk-sales.
Any source code or other supplementary material referenced by the author in this book is available to readers on GitHub. For more detailed information, please visit https://www.apress.com/gp/services/source-code.

If disposing of this product, please recycle the paper.

To my beloved daughter, Mansi, whose laughter and curiosity light up my world and inspire every word on these pages. Your boundless energy and inquisitive spirit are the driving force behind my endeavors.

To my esteemed parents, whose unwavering support, wisdom, and love have been the foundation upon which all my achievements stand. Your sacrifices and guidance have been instrumental in shaping the person I am today.

To the pioneering researchers in the field of data analytics, whose relentless pursuit of knowledge and innovation continues to push the boundaries of what is possible. Your dedication to advancing our understanding in this ever-evolving field is both admirable and essential.

With deepest gratitude and respect,

Ramchandra S Mangrulkar
Pallavi Vijay Chavan

Contents

About the Author

Dr. Ramchandra Sharad Mangrulkar is a Professor in the Department of Information Technology at Dwarkadas J. Sanghvi College of Engineering in Mumbai, India. He holds various memberships in professional organizations such as IEEE, ISTE, ACM, and IACSIT. He has established himself as a knowledgeable and skilled professional in his field. He has also obtained certifications like Certified Network Security Specialist (ICSI – CNSS) from ICSI, UK. He has a strong publication record with 126 publications. Dr. Mangrulkar is proficient in several technologies and tools, including Microsoft's Power BI, Power Automate, Power Query, Power Virtual Agents, Google's Dialog Flow, Data Analytics Models, and Overleaf.

Dr. Pallavi Vijay Chavan is an Associate Professor in the Department of Information Technology at Ramrao Adik Institute of Technology, D Y Patil Deemed to be University, Navi Mumbai, MH, India. She has been in academics since the past 17 years and has worked in the areas of computing theory, data science, data analytics, and network security. In her academic journey, she has published research work in the data science and security domains with reputed publishers, including Springer, Elsevier, CRC Press, and Inderscience.

About the Technical Reviewer

 **Dr. Parikshit** is a senior member of IEEE and is Professor and Dean of Research and Development at Vishwakarma Institute of Technology, Pune, India. Prior to this, he worked as Dean of Research and Development and Head of the Department of Artificial Intelligence and Data Science at Vishwakarma Institute of Information Technology, Pune, India, and Professor and Head of the Department of Computer Engineering at Sinhgad Institutes. He completed his PhD from Aalborg University, Denmark, and continued as Postdoc Researcher at CMI, Copenhagen, Denmark. He has 24 years of teaching and research experience. He is the chairman of the Board of Studies of AI & DS at VIIT and an ex-member of the Board of Studies in Computer Engineering and ex-chairman in Information Technology, Savitribai Phule Pune University, and various universities and autonomous colleges across India. He has 26 patents and 200+ research publications (Google Scholar citations are 3500+ with H-index of 26, Scopus citations are 19,200+ with H-index of 21, and Web of Science citations are 528 with H-index of 11) and authored/edited 62 books with Springer, CRC Press, Cambridge University Press, etc. He is Editor in Chief for IGI Global (*International Journal of Rough Sets and Data Analysis* and *Inderscience International Journal of Grid and Utility Computing*), Associate Editor for IGI Global (*Journal of Affective Computing and Human Interfaces (JACHI)*), member of the Editorial Review Board for IGI Global (*International Journal of Ambient Computing and Intelligence*), and reviewer for various transactions, journals, and

conferences of the repute. His research interests are machine learning, data science, algorithms, Internet of Things, identity management, and security. He is guiding eight PhD students in the area of IoT and machine learning, and six students have successfully defended their PhD under his supervision from SPPU. He is also the recipient of "Best Faculty Award" by Sinhgad Institutes and Cognizant Technologies Solutions, International Level S4DS Distinguished Researcher of the Year 2023, and State Level Meritorious Teacher Award. He has delivered 200+ lectures at national and international levels. His book on design and analysis of algorithms is referred as textbook in IIITs and NITs, and his book "Data Analytics for Pandemics" by CRC Press has received two international awards in 2020.

Acknowledgments

I extend my heartfelt gratitude to the management of our esteemed institution, whose vision and leadership have provided the robust framework within which this work was conceived and realized. Your commitment to excellence and innovation has been a constant source of inspiration.

A special note of thanks to the principal of our institution, whose unwavering support and encouragement have been pivotal throughout this journey. Your guidance has been instrumental in navigating the complexities of this project, ensuring its successful completion.

To our diligent undergraduate students, I am deeply appreciative of your dedication and hard work. Your insightful assignments and lab work have significantly enriched this endeavor. The fruitful discussions we've shared have been invaluable, sparking new ideas and perspectives that have greatly enhanced the depth of this work.

I am also profoundly grateful to the SAS team, whose expertise and collaboration have been indispensable. Your technical acumen and problem-solving skills have been critical in overcoming numerous challenges encountered along the way.

Lastly, I acknowledge the developers of programming languages in data science and R. Your innovative tools and frameworks have provided the essential foundation upon which much of this research is built. Your contributions to the field are both groundbreaking and transformative.

With sincere appreciation,

Ramchandra S Mangrulkar
Pallavi Vijay Chavan

Introduction to Analytics

1

Analytics Overview

What Is Analytics? Why Do We Need Analytics? Analytics in Decision-Making, Game Changers and Innovators, Power of Analytics, Predictive Analytics, Predicting, Predicting Binary Outcomes, Trees and Other Predictive Models, Experts View on Analytics, Finance, Manufacturing, Healthcare, Telecommunications, Supply Chain, Digital Analytics, Information Technology

1.1 Analytics Overview

Analytics is the process of identifying, understanding, and conveying important trends in data. It allows us to see insights and meaningful facts that we might otherwise overlook. Business analytics focuses on using data insights to create better decisions that will assist firms in increasing sales, lowering costs, and making other business changes.

We need analytics because it helps firms improve their performance by evaluating data and making better decisions. It facilitates the use of more data to generate deeper insights faster, for a greater number of people, and for a lower cost. Analytics is critical for organizations to achieve their objectives, empower people to perform self-service analysis, and take action based on findings.

Analytics has a long history, dating back to ancient times. Notable milestones include William Playfair's conception of the bar chart in 1785, Charles Joseph Minard's visualization of Napoleon's army losses in 1812, and Herman Hollerith's invention of the tabulating machine in 1890. These developments helped shape analytics into the process we know today.

Analytics has evolved since the introduction of relational databases, Standard Query Language (SQL), data warehouses, and business intelligence tools. The

© Ramchandra S Mangrulkar and Pallavi Vijay Chavan 2025
R. S. Mangrulkar and P. Vijay Chavan, *Predictive Analytics with SAS and R*,
https://doi.org/10.1007/979-8-8688-0905-7_1

concept of data mining first appeared in the 1990s, allowing firms to evaluate patterns in enormous databases. Analytics technologies are increasingly advanced, allowing for a broader transformation of corporate knowledge through automation and real-time data processing.

This book is designed for students and practitioners who want to improve their knowledge of predictive analytics. The training will also prepare students for careers in data analytics. If you're looking for the best competitive strategy to help your company succeed, join us to learn how to use predictive analytics.

Analytics is an essential tool for businesses, accelerating economic growth and delivering useful insights. Professor Dinesh Kumar from the Indian Institute of Management Bangalore introduces the Predictive Analytics course, emphasizing the relevance of analytics in decision-making and the advantages it provides to businesses.

He begins by referencing Edward Deming, emphasizing the importance of statistics in decision-making. This quotation emphasizes the need of data and analytics in influencing organizational decisions, particularly when confronted with the "Hippo Algorithm," in which decisions are frequently affected by the highest paid person's opinions.

The business context is critical since it determines the success of analytics by posing the appropriate questions. Prof. Kumar demonstrates this using Target's pregnancy test instance, in which analytics helped identify price-insensitive clients early on, resulting in significant value creation.

Analytics relies heavily on technology, particularly with large data, which necessitates complex tools and systems for data collection, storage, retrieval, and analysis.

The science component of analytics entails solving classification problems using algorithms such as logistic regression, decision trees, random forest, and neural networks, as in the Target example of identifying pregnant clients.

1.2   Why Analytics

Analytics is critical for organizations since it aids in a variety of tasks, such as eliminating inefficiencies, issue solving, decision-making, driving innovation, and creating a competitive advantage. Here's an explanation of why analytics is important:

- **Removing inefficiencies:** Organizations use analytics, like Six Sigma, to improve processes and eliminate inefficiencies. Starting with easy wins can set the stage for more complex analytics projects.
- **Problem-solving:** Analytics helps solve specific problems, such as reducing inventory costs for a manufacturing company, by predicting demand accurately.
- **Decision-making:** Analytics provides data-backed insights that aid organizations in making informed decisions. For example, determining the right discount for retail products based on inventory and sell-through rate.

- **Driving innovation:** Many innovative products and services, like Amazon Go and Google Maps, are driven by analytics. However, only a small percentage of organizations currently use analytics for innovation.
- **Competitive strategy:** Companies like Google, Amazon, and Procter & Gamble use analytics as a competitive strategy to stay ahead in the market.

The primary goal of analytics is to assist in decision-making, as human decision-making is often flawed. This is demonstrated by the Monty Hall Problem, where people tend to make suboptimal decisions even when presented with simple choices.

In real-world scenarios, the complexity of decision-making increases significantly, making it challenging for human brains to find the best solutions without the help of analytics. For example, Walmart's scale is so vast that if it were a country, its GDP would rank 28th in the world. Similarly, Amazon faces complex logistical challenges, such as the traveling salesman problem, which analytics helps solve efficiently.

1.3 Predictive Analytics

Decision-makers frequently grapple with problems like, "What is the right price for a product?", "Which consumer is most likely to default on their loan repayment?", "What products should you recommend to an existing customer?" Finding the appropriate answers to these questions can be both tough and gratifying.

Predictive analytics is growing as a competitive approach in a variety of industries, with the potential to distinguish high-performing businesses. It seeks to forecast the likelihood of a future event, such as customer churn, loan defaults, and stock market swings, resulting in successful corporate management.

Predictive analytics models commonly include multiple linear regression, logistic regression, Autoregressive Integrated Moving Average (ARIMA), decision trees, and neural networks. Regression models help us understand the relationships between these variables and how they might be used to make decisions.

The process can be summarized in Figure 1-1.

1.3.1 Why Do We Need Analytics?

Analytics is critical for transforming raw data into relevant insights that enable firms to make sound decisions. Previously, analytics enabled firms to measure performance metrics and identify previous trends, allowing for more effective strategic planning. Analytics has grown to encompass advanced techniques such as machine learning and predictive modeling, which enable businesses to predict future trends, optimize operations, and improve consumer experiences. The ability to evaluate large amounts of data in real time has become a significant competitive advantage in the digital age.

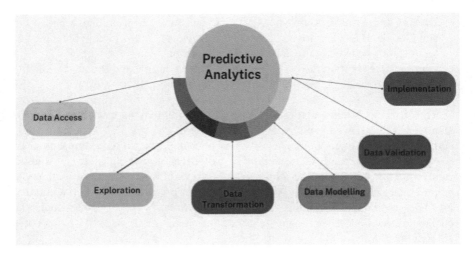

Figure 1-1. Predictive analytics process

The benefits of analytics are numerous and growing. Historically, organizations employed analytics to improve financial reporting and operational efficiency, resulting in cost savings and increased production. Currently, analytics fosters innovation by offering insights into customer behavior, enabling targeted marketing, and encouraging data-driven decision-making across all industries. It helps with risk management by recognizing abnormalities and predicting possible problems before they worsen, so sparing enterprises from substantial losses. Furthermore, analytics promotes regulatory compliance by ensuring that data is appropriately reported and monitored.

However, implementing analytics is not without its problems. Data privacy concerns, the complexities of integrating diverse data sources, and the necessity for qualified individuals to understand data are all important barriers. Analytics can address these problems by providing powerful data encryption methods, seamless integration platforms, and user-friendly visualization tools that make data interpretation easier. Furthermore, analytics may improve decision-making by offering actionable insights via artificial intelligence and automation, decreasing the need for human analysis and assisting firms in staying nimble in a fast-changing environment.

1.3.2   Game-Changing Innovations

Many businesses have effectively used analytics to guide their goals and operations. These examples demonstrate the many applications of analytics across industries. Google created a page ranking algorithm called Markov Chain, which revolutionized search engine effectiveness. Procter and Gamble (P&G) uses analytics as a competitive strategy to compete with private labels, analyzing massive amounts of data and making informed decisions. Target is well known for its efficient use of analytics, such as forecasting client pregnancy based on shopping trends. Every day, Capital One runs a number of algorithms to determine which customers are the most profitable. Hewlett-Packard developed a flight risk score to help retain prized talent by identifying individuals who are likely to quit. Obama's 2012 presidential campaign used persuasion modeling to target indecisive voters.

Netflix had a 1% root mean squared error in forecasting consumer ratings for movies and held a competition to enhance the system. Amazon relies heavily on analytics for product recommendations, which account for 35% of sales. OkCupid predicts message responses using data on their online dating site. Polyphonic HMI created Hit Songs Signs, a model that predicts the success of songs before they are released. These examples demonstrate the breadth of analytics applications, ranging from enhancing search engine algorithms to predicting musical success. Studies have found a strong link between an organization's analytics sophistication and its competitive success, highlighting the relevance of analytics in today's business world.

1.3.3 Types of Analytics

There are various sorts of data analytics, each with a different aim and offering unique insights. Here are some of the major types:

1. **Descriptive analytics:** Descriptive analytics is the most fundamental type of analytics, serving as the foundation for all others. It allows you to recognize patterns in unprocessed data and provide a quick explanation of previous or current events.

   "What happened?" is addressed by descriptive analytics.

   Let's say, for instance, that you are examining the data of your business and discover a seasonal uptick in sales of a certain product – a video game system. Descriptive analytics can tell you this: "Every year, sales of this video game console rise in October, November, and early December."

   > Descriptive analytics
   >
   > Descriptive analytics is concerned with condensing, analyzing, and presenting historical data.

2. **Diagnostic analytics:** "Why did this happen?" is the next logical question that diagnostic analytics attempts to answer.

   This form of analysis goes one step further by comparing concurrent trends or movements, finding correlations between variables, and, when feasible, establishing causal linkages.

Using the previous example, you may conduct demographic research on video game console users and determine that they are primarily between the ages of eight and eighteen. Clients' average ages range from 35 to 55. According to data from consumer surveys, one of the most common reasons people buy video game systems is for their children. The Christmas season, which includes gift-giving, could explain the increase in sales in the fall and early winter.

> **Diagnostic analytics**
>
> Diagnostic analytics is the practice of analyzing data to identify the causes of trends and the relationships between variables. It can be thought of as the obvious next step after utilizing descriptive analytics to find trends.

3. **Predictive analytics:** Predictive analytics provides a solution to the question "What might happen in the future?" by forecasting future trends or events.

   You may forecast what the future may hold for your business by examining past data in conjunction with market trends.

   For example, you have plenty of information to forecast that, as in the previous ten years, sales of video game consoles have peaked around October, November, and early December. Supported by positive tendencies in the video gaming sector overall, this forecast seems sensible.

   Anticipating future events might assist your company in developing plans based on expected outcomes.

4. **Prescriptive analytics:** In prescriptive analytics, the query "What should we do next?" is addressed. Prescriptive analytics considers every aspect of a situation and makes recommendations for practical solutions. This kind of analytics can be quite helpful when making judgments based on data.

   To conclude the video game example, what course of action should your team take in light of the anticipated seasonality pattern resulting from the winter gift-giving season? Let's say you choose to do an A/B test with two commercials, one aimed at consumers (their parents) and the other at the product's end users, children. How to further profit from the seasonal rise and its purported source can be determined by analyzing the test's results. Alternatively, you may choose to step up your marketing in September and use holiday-themed message in an attempt to sustain the surge for an additional month.

   Although manual prescriptive analysis is feasible and accessible, machine learning algorithms are frequently used to assist in sifting through massive amounts of data in order to suggest the best course of action. "If" and "else" phrases are used by algorithms as rules for parsing data. An algorithm suggests one line of action if a certain set of conditions is satisfied. Even though the assertions only cover a small portion of machine learning algorithms, they are essential to algorithm training along with mathematical equations.

Table 1-1. Difference Between Predictive and Descriptive Analytics

Sr. No.	Aspect	Predictive Analytics	Descriptive Analytics
1	Objective	Predict future outcomes based on historical data	Understand past and present data to identify trends and patterns
2	Techniques Used	Machine learning, statistical modeling, data mining	Data aggregation, data summarization, data visualization
3	Examples	Forecasting sales, predicting customer churn, risk assessment	Sales reports, customer segmentation, performance dashboards
4	Output	Probabilistic forecasts, risk scores, predictive models	Summary statistics, charts, graphs, historical insights
5	Data Used	Historical data, real-time data, external data sources	Historical data, transactional data, operational data

> **Prescriptive analytics**
>
> Prescriptive analytics provides solutions to the question "What should we do?" by recommending actions to achieve desired outcomes based on predictions of future events or trends.

Table 1-1 gives the difference between predictive analytics and descriptive analytics.

1.4 Predictive Analytics

Companies utilize predictive analytics to address a variety of issues, including recognizing customer churn, projecting customer purchases for recommender systems, and forecasting credit risk. The first stage of the framework is problem characterization and opportunity identification, which are critical for influencing the organization's top or bottom line. For example, Bigbasket.com employs a "Did you forget" function to remind consumers of things they may have neglected to add to their cart, lowering logistical expenses and increasing revenue. The second step is data collecting, which is typically difficult due to low data quality. Data preparation entails addressing missing data and feature engineering to provide new variables for better prediction.

The data is then divided into training and validation sets to facilitate model building and testing. Several models are created to determine the best one depending on stated criteria. Results are communicated, and the model is deployed, which is commonly done through dashboards and new features. Machine learning is a subset of artificial intelligence that encompasses supervised, unsupervised, reinforcement, and evolutionary learning methods. These algorithms are applied based on the presence of outcome variables in the dataset. This course only covers a subset of predictive analytics; for more information, see the book *Business Analytics: The Science of Data-Driven Decision Making*, released by Wiley in 2017.

> **Prescriptive analytics**
>
> Predictive analytics is a way of using data to foresee future events and outcomes, such as customer behavior, market trends, or machine failures.

1.5   Predicting

Predictive analytics, an important talent for anticipating events, has a long history based on statistical approaches and data analysis. The term "predictive analytics" became popular in the late 20th century, but the discipline has a considerably longer history. Early examples include Thomas Bayes' work in probability theory in the 18th century and Francis Galton's regression analysis in the 19th century. These fundamental concepts were later employed in a variety of industries to estimate demand, manage risk, and optimize operations. For example, in the early 1900s, weather forecasting began to use predictive models based on historical data, and during World War II, Alan Turing used statistical approaches to crack the Enigma code, demonstrating the usefulness of predictive analytics in decision-making and strategy. Table 1-2 gives the category of problems that can be solved using Predictive Analytics.

1.5.1   Predicting Binary Outcomes

Binary outcome prediction is the art of predicting whether or not an event will occur. Sorting examples into one of two classes or categories is the objective of classifying problems, which is how this might be presented in many cases.

Table 1-2. Problems That Can and Cannot Be Solved Using Predictive Analytics

Problems that can be solved	Problems that cannot be solved
Predicting customer churn	Identifying the exact reason for customer dissatisfaction
Forecasting sales for the next quarter	Determining the impact of a new competitor entering the market
Personalizing marketing campaigns based on customer behavior	Understanding the emotional state of a customer
Predicting equipment failures based on usage patterns	Guaranteeing 100% accuracy in predictions
Detecting fraudulent transactions in real time	Eliminating all fraud

For instance, a binary outcome prediction challenge in healthcare is determining a patient's likelihood of contracting a specific disease based on their medical history and other variables. Predicting whether a customer will default on a loan can also be thought of as a binary outcome prediction task in the finance industry. Binary outcome prediction is a frequent use of machine learning methods, including logistic regression, decision trees, random forests, and support vector machines. These algorithms use the data to identify patterns, then use those patterns to forecast future events.

Evaluation metrics are used to evaluate the effectiveness of binary outcome prediction models, including accuracy, precision, recall, and F1-score. The model's predictive ability for the positive and negative classes is assessed using these criteria.

1.5.2 Examples

The following examples give the idea of predicting binary outcomes.

Example 1: Churn prediction
Suppose a telecom company wants to predict whether a customer will churn based on their usage patterns. They collect data on the number of calls made per month (*calls*), the duration of calls (*call_duration*), and the customer's monthly bill (*monthly_bill*).

Using logistic regression, a model is given as

$$\text{Churn Probability} = \frac{1}{1 + e^{-(\beta_0 + \beta_1 \times \text{calls} + \beta_2 \times \text{call\_duration} + \beta_3 \times \text{monthly\_bill})}}$$

where

- β_0 is the intercept term
- $\beta_1, \beta_2, \beta_3$ are the coefficients

If the churn probability is greater than 0.5, the customer is predicted to churn.

The Python code for the above example:

```python
import pandas as pd
from sklearn.model_selection import train_test_split
from sklearn.linear_model import LogisticRegression
from sklearn.metrics import accuracy_score

# Sample data
data = {
    'calls': [80, 120, 180, 210, 250],
    'call_duration': [40, 60, 90, 100, 120],
    'monthly_bill': [40, 50, 70, 75, 85],
    'churn': [0, 1, 0, 1, 1]   # 0 for no churn, 1 for churn
}
```

```
13
14 df = pd.DataFrame(data)
15
16 # Split data into training and test sets
17 X = df[['calls', 'call_duration', 'monthly_bill']]
18 Y = df['churn']
19 x_train, x_test, y_train, y_test = train_test_split(X, Y,
       test_size=0.2, random_state=42)
20
21 # Train logistic regression model
22 model = LogisticRegression()
23 model.fit(x_train, y_train)
24
25 # Make predictions
26 y_pred = model.predict(x_test)
27
28 # Calculate accuracy
29 accuracy = accuracy_score(y_test, y_pred)
30 print(f'Accuracy: {accuracy}')
31
32 # Predict churn probability for a new customer
33 new_customer = [[200, 100, 65]]    # Calls: 200, Call duration:
       100, Monthly bill: 65
34 churn_probability = model.predict_proba(new_customer)[0][1]
35 print(f'Churn Probability: {churn_probability}')
```

To execute the above code, use any Python editor, say VS Code, and paste the code. To compile, make sure to run the following two commands on the VS Code command prompt:

```
1
2 PS C:\Users\ramchandra.m\Desktop\Deep Learning> pip install
       scikit-learn
3
4 PS C:\Users\ramchandra.m\Desktop\Deep Learning> python.exe -m
       pip install --upgrade pip
```

The probable output is

```
1
2 Churn Probability: 0.8154274015593822
```

Example 2: Fraud detection
A bank wants to predict whether a transaction is fraudulent based on transaction amount (*amount*), location (*location*), and time of day (*time*).

Using the logistic regression model, a model is given as

$$\text{Fraud Probability} = \frac{1}{1 + e^{-(\beta_0 + \beta_1 \times \text{amount} + \beta_2 \times \text{location} + \beta_3 \times \text{time})}}$$

If the fraud probability is greater than 0.5, the transaction is predicted to be fraudulent.

Python code for the above example:

```
from sklearn.linear_model import LogisticRegression
from sklearn.model_selection import train_test_split
import numpy as np

# Sample data
X = np.array([[100, 1, 8], [200, 0, 15], [300, 1, 21]])
y = np.array([0, 1, 0])

# Split the data into training and test sets
X_train, X_test, y_train, y_test = train_test_split(X, y,
    test_size=0.2, random_state=42)

# Fit the logistic regression model
model = LogisticRegression()
model.fit(X_train, y_train)

# Print the predicted probabilities
fraud_probability = model.predict_proba(X_test)[:, 1].mean()
print("Fraud Probability:", fraud_probability)
```

Example 3: Employee attrition
An HR department wants to predict whether an employee will leave the company based on their performance rating (*performance*), years of experience (*experience*), and salary (*salary*).

Using the logistic regression, a model is given as

$$\text{Attrition Probability} = \frac{1}{1 + e^{-(\beta_0 + \beta_1 \times \text{performance} + \beta_2 \times \text{experience} + \beta_3 \times \text{salary})}}$$

If the attrition probability is greater than 0.5, the employee is predicted to leave the company.

In each example, the coefficients β_0, β_1, β_2, β_3 are estimated from the data using logistic regression, and the predicted probabilities are used to make binary predictions. Python code for the above example:

```
from sklearn.linear_model import LogisticRegression
import numpy as np

# Sample data
X = np.array([[8, 2, 50000], [6, 5, 60000], [7, 3, 55000],
    [9, 1, 48000]])
y = np.array([1, 0, 1, 0])  # 1 for leaving, 0 for not
    leaving
```

```
 7
 8  # Adjusting the salary to change the predicted probability to
      0.5
 9  X[0, 2] = 65500  # Increase salary for the first employee
10
11  # Fit the logistic regression model
12  model = LogisticRegression()
13  model.fit(X, y)
14
15  # Predict the probability of attrition for the first employee
16  attrition_probability = model.predict_proba([X[0]])[:, 1][0]
17  print("Adjusted Salary for Probability 0.5:", X[0, 2])
18  print("Attrition Probability:", attrition_probability)
```

1.5.3   Trees and Other Predictive Models

Predictive analytics models are designed to evaluate past data, find patterns, analyze trends, and forecast future developments.

These predictive analytics solutions are powered by a variety of models and algorithms suited to a wide range of use cases. Identifying the best predictive modeling methodologies for a specific business is critical for maximizing the benefits of a predictive analytics solution and using data to make educated decisions. For example, a store attempting to reduce customer turnover would require different predictive analytics models than a hospital anticipating the number of emergency department admissions in the following ten days.

The Classification Model
The categorization model is one of the most straightforward types of predictive analytics models. It categorizes data using insights gained from historical data.

When it comes to addressing binary questions, classification models excel at offering comprehensive insights that are helpful in decision-making. These models are able to answer queries such as the following.

"Is this customer about to churn?" is a question for a store. A lender's question is "Will this loan be approved?" and "Is this applicant likely to default?" "Is this a fraudulent transaction?" is a question for an online bank. The categorization model may be used in a range of industries because of its versatility and ability to be readily retrained with new data.

Many methods can be used to mathematically characterize a classification predictive model; logistic regression is a popular and useful approach.

Example: Representation of a logistic regression model

In logistic regression, the probability P of a binary outcome Y (where Y can be 0 or 1) given a set of predictors (features) $X_1, X_2, \ldots, X_n$ is modeled using the logistic function:

$$P(Y = 1 \mid X) = \sigma(Z) = \frac{1}{1 + e^{-Z}} \tag{1-1}$$

where $Z = \beta_0 + \beta_1 X_1 + \beta_2 X_2 + \ldots + \beta_n X_n$

Here, β_0 is the intercept, and $\beta_1, \beta_2, \ldots, \beta_n$ are the coefficients corresponding to each predictor.

Clustering Model

The clustering model divides data into distinct, nested smart groups based on comparable characteristics. If an online shoe firm wants to conduct targeted marketing campaigns for their clients, they can sift through hundreds of thousands of records to develop a personalized approach for each individual. But is this the best use of time? Probably not. Using the clustering methodology, companies may swiftly categorize customers into comparable groups based on shared traits and develop larger-scale plans for each.

This predictive modeling technique might also be used to divide loan applicants into "smart buckets" based on loan qualities, identify crime-prone zones in a city, and benchmark SaaS customer data to detect worldwide patterns of use.

Example: Representation of a clustering model

In clustering, the goal is to partition a set of data points into clusters, where each cluster consists of data points that are more similar to each other than to those in other clusters. One common method is the k-means clustering algorithm, which aims to minimize the within-cluster sum of squares (WCSS).

The k-means algorithm proceeds as follows:

1. Initialize k cluster centroids randomly.
2. Assign each data point X_i to the nearest centroid based on the Euclidean distance.
3. Update each centroid to be the mean of the points assigned to it.

The objective function that k-means seeks to minimize is

$$J = \sum_{i=1}^{k} \sum_{j=1}^{n_i} \|X_j^{(i)} - \mu_i\|^2 \tag{1-2}$$

where k is the number of clusters, n_i is the number of points in cluster i, $X_j^{(i)}$ is the j-th point in cluster i, and μ_i is the centroid of cluster i.

Here, $\|X_j^{(i)} - \mu_i\|$ represents the Euclidean distance between a point $X_j^{(i)}$ and the cluster centroid μ_i. The algorithm iterates between the assignment and update steps until convergence, i.e., until the assignments no longer change or the decrease in the objective function becomes negligible.

Forecast Model

The forecast model, one of the most popular predictive analytics methods, is concerned with metric value prediction, which involves forecasting numeric values for new data based on prior data.

This model can be used anywhere historical numerical data is available. The scenarios include the following: A SaaS company can forecast how many customers it is likely to convert in a single week. A call center can forecast the number of support calls it will receive every hour. A shoe store can determine how much inventory it should keep on hand to meet demand during a specific sales period. The forecast model takes into account many input parameters. If a restaurant owner wishes to anticipate how many customers they will receive in the coming week, the model will consider aspects such as: Is there an event nearby? What's the weather forecast? Is there an illness going around?

Example: Representation of a forecasting model

In forecasting, the goal is to predict future values of a time series based on its historical data. One common method for time series forecasting is the ARIMA (Autoregressive Integrated Moving Average) model.

The ARIMA model is defined by three parameters: p, d, and q. p is the number of lag observations (autoregressive part), d is the number of times the raw observations are differenced (differencing part), and q is the size of the moving average window (moving average part).

The ARIMA model equation is

$$Y_t = c + \phi_1 Y_{t-1} + \phi_2 Y_{t-2} + \ldots + \phi_p Y_{t-p} + \theta_1 \epsilon_{t-1} + \theta_2 \epsilon_{t-2} + \ldots$$
$$+ \theta_q \epsilon_{t-q} + \epsilon_t \tag{1-3}$$

where Y_t is the actual value at time t, c is a constant, $\phi_1, \phi_2, \ldots, \phi_p$ are the coefficients for the autoregressive terms, $\theta_1, \theta_2, \ldots, \theta_q$ are the coefficients for the moving average terms, and ϵ_t is the error term at time t.

The ARIMA model proceeds as follows:

1. **Identification:** Determine the values of p, d, and q based on the autocorrelation function (ACF) and partial autocorrelation function (PACF) plots.
2. **Estimation:** Estimate the parameters ϕ and θ using historical data.
3. **Diagnostic checking:** Validate the model by checking the residuals to ensure they resemble white noise.
4. **Forecasting:** Use the fitted model to predict future values of the time series.

The ARIMA model can be extended to seasonal data (SARIMA) by incorporating seasonal terms. This model is widely used for its flexibility and ability to handle a variety of time series patterns.

1.6 Data Sources and Collection Methods

In the age of big data and predictive analytics, selecting data sources and collecting methods is critical to developing strong, trustworthy, and insightful prediction models. This section digs into the many data sources and gathering methods used in predictive analytics, particularly in relation to big data and data lakes.

Predictive analytics leverages statistical algorithms and machine learning techniques to identify the likelihood of future outcomes based on historical data. The accuracy and effectiveness of predictive models heavily rely on the quality and variety of data sources, as well as the methods used to collect this data. In big data environments and data lakes, data collection is often complex due to the volume, variety, and velocity of the data involved.

1.6.1 Types of Data Sources

In analytics, data can be categorized into several types, each offering unique insights into different aspects. Understanding these types of data sources is essential for comprehensive analysis and informed decision-making.

Structured Data
Structured data is data that is organized in a preset format, usually in rows and columns. Examples include relational databases, spreadsheets, and data warehouses. Structured data is simple to analyze and alter, making it a popular option for predictive analytics.

Unstructured Data
Text documents, photos, videos, and social media information are examples of unstructured data, which lacks a set format. This type of data is becoming more valuable in predictive analytics due to its richness and depth. Natural language processing (NLP) and picture recognition are methods for extracting meaningful information from unstructured data.

Semi-structured Data
Semi-structured data is a combination of structured and unstructured data in which the information is not stored in a relational database but retains some organizational qualities, such as XML and JSON. This data format is frequently seen in online data, log files, and NoSQL databases.

1.6.2 Data Collection Methods

Data collection in analytics involves various methods, each suited to capturing different types of data crucial for comprehensive analysis and insight generation.

Real-Time Data Collection

Real-time data gathering entails recording information as it is generated. This approach is critical for applications that require quick analysis and response, such as fraud detection and stock market forecasting. Apache Kafka and Apache Flink are frequently used for real-time data processing in big data contexts.

Batch Data Collection

Batch data collection entails gathering and processing data in huge chunks at regular times. This strategy is appropriate for scenarios that do not require real-time data, such as end-of-day reporting and periodic trend analysis. Hadoop and Spark are widely used solutions for batch processing in data lakes.

API-Based Data Collection

APIs enable systems to communicate and exchange data. API-based data collection is commonly used to integrate several systems and acquire information from external sources such as social media platforms, meteorological services, and financial markets. This strategy keeps the data up to date and easy to retrieve.

Sensor and IoT Data Collection

The Internet of Things (IoT) is a network of linked devices that collect and share data. Sensor-based data collecting is employed in a number of areas, including healthcare, manufacturing, and transportation. Data from IoT devices is frequently high volume and real time, making it ideal for predictive analytics in big data settings.

1.6.3   Data Lakes As a Collection Platform

Data lakes provide a single repository for structured, semi-structured, and unstructured data of any size. Unlike typical databases, data lakes may store a wide range of data kinds and sources, making them perfect for big data analytics. Data lakes are widely built and managed using technologies like Apache Hadoop and Amazon S3.

Advantages of Data Lakes
- **Scalability:** Data lakes can scale to accommodate large volumes of data from multiple sources.
- **Flexibility:** They can store diverse data types without the need for a predefined schema.
- **Cost-effectiveness:** Data lakes offer cost-effective storage solutions compared to traditional databases.
- **Advanced analytics:** They support advanced analytics and machine learning by providing a rich dataset for model training.

Challenges of Data Lakes
- **Data quality:** Ensuring data quality and consistency can be challenging due to the diverse nature of data sources.
- **Governance:** Implementing effective data governance and security measures is critical to protect sensitive information.
- **Complexity:** Managing and processing large-scale data requires sophisticated tools and expertise.

1.7 Case Studies and Expert Opinion on Analytics

Data analytics trends are always changing. With new technology breakthroughs, data analytics is likely to continue its rising trend in 2023. In this era of rapid corporate expansion, data collection and analysis are vital for businesses to stay competitive.

Data science, artificial intelligence, and big data analytics are three key themes in today's data-driven economy. In this data analytics interview series, we delve deeply into the newest trends and scope for 2023. Experts indicate that real-time data visualization will be a critical component in the future of data analytics, as well as the skills required for success as data analysts.

1.7.1 Finance

Data analytics has evolved into a vital tool for financial businesses, allowing them to better monitor and anticipate their finances. The coronavirus epidemic has highlighted the importance of advanced data analytics in navigating the unpredictability in the banking sector. According to Bassem Hamdy, understanding data analytics enables businesses to estimate cash flow and carry out strategic financial objectives, providing long-term service to their markets and clientele. Implementing a financial strategy necessitates a thorough understanding of the company's financial status, which may be obtained through the services of financial data analytics experts.

Data analytics is altering the banking industry by eliminating human error in day-to-day transactions and allowing executives to turn data into meaningful insights. It helps financial teams obtain a comprehensive understanding of key performance indicators (KPIs), such as sales, net income, and payroll costs. Finance teams can improve their ability to spot fraud and understand revenue turnover by studying key data. The increase in digital fraud activities in 2020 emphasizes the value of data analytics in ensuring financial integrity and security.

Big data has considerably enhanced stock market operations and investment decision-making processes. It gives finance professionals the tools they need to examine massive datasets, allowing them to make more informed and accurate decisions. The capacity to transform organized and unstructured data into meaningful insights is critical for effective decision-making and strategic planning. As financial services grow, data analytics will play an increasingly important role in identifying trends, detecting fraud, and improving operational efficiency.

The following subsections give some of the case studies that a reader can explore.

Case Study: Enhancing Fraud Detection at a Major Bank
A large international bank encountered several difficulties in identifying fraudulent activity among the many transactions that occurred every day. The bank used cutting-edge data analytics methods to counter this. Through the application of machine learning algorithms and real-time data analysis, the bank was able to discern abnormalities and strange patterns that suggested possible fraudulent activity. The bank's financial losses from fraudulent activity were much decreased thanks to this system's quick detection and reaction times. By offering a strong foundation for continuing fraud prevention, the bank was also able to better comply with regulatory obligations thanks to the use of analytics.

Case Study: Optimizing Investment Strategies with Predictive Analytics
Using predictive analytics, an investment business aimed to improve portfolio management. To predict market trends and asset performance, the company created predictive models by examining past market data and a range of economic variables. With the use of these models, the company was able to optimize its investment strategies and dynamically modify portfolios in response to anticipated changes in the market. Consequently, the company realized increased investment returns and enhanced risk mitigation. Predictive analytics adoption improved decision-making procedures and gave clients more dependable and transparent investing possibilities.

Enhancing Customer Experience Through Personalization
A local bank sought to enhance its clientele's experience by providing individualized services. The bank examined consumer data, including transaction histories, behavior patterns, and preferences, using data analytics. The bank was able to develop customized marketing campaigns and financial products based on the demands of each customer thanks to this analysis. Customers who traveled regularly, for instance, were sent personalized offers for credit cards with travel incentives and travel insurance. Customer engagement and happiness increased significantly as a result of the personalization initiatives, and cross-selling potential increased by 15%. The bank was able to increase business growth and cultivate better client relationships thanks to data analytics.

1.7.2 Manufacturing

With the growth of Industry 4.0 and smart factories, industrial analytics has become critical for staying competitive. The global market for smart manufacturing solutions is expected to grow to $650 billion by 2029. Manufacturing analytics uses technology like IIoT sensors, cloud computing, and machine learning to deliver real-time data, allowing manufacturers to optimize operations, improve quality control, and reduce downtime through predictive maintenance.

Manufacturing analytics provides several advantages, including increased operational efficiency, greater quality control, and streamlined supply chain management. End-to-end visibility aids in early detection of faults, defect reduction, and improved inventory management. Predictive maintenance, real-time quality monitoring, production planning, and inventory optimization are all examples of applications that help businesses make data-driven decisions that boost profitability and operational effectiveness.

To effectively profit from manufacturing analytics, businesses must install integrated software systems that can collect, analyze, and visualize data from multiple sources. Data connectivity, edge and cloud analytics, artificial intelligence and machine learning, and enhanced visualization tools are all essential competencies. With the appropriate skills, manufacturers can modernize their processes, increase revenue, and remain competitive in today's industrial world. Andromeda Technology Solutions specializes in assisting manufacturers with implementing these technologies to improve their operations and performance.

The following subsections give some of the case studies that a reader can explore.

Case Study: Reducing Downtime with Predictive Maintenance

Unexpected equipment failures plagued a sizable auto manufacturing facility, causing expensive downtime and causing production timetables to be thrown off. The plant used machine learning algorithms and Industrial Internet of Things (IIoT) sensors to build predictive maintenance analytics in order to address this. These tools used real-time equipment monitoring and data analysis to identify possible problems before they happened. The company greatly increased the lifespan of crucial machinery and decreased unplanned downtime by thirty percent by proactively scheduling maintenance based on predictive data. This strategy reduced maintenance and repair costs significantly while simultaneously increasing operational efficiency.

Case Study: Enhancing Quality Control with Real-Time Data

A producer of consumer electronics sought to decrease production line problems and raise the caliber of its products. Sensor data collected during manufacturing could be analyzed by the manufacturer through the integration of real-time monitoring systems and advanced data analytics. This made it possible to identify abnormalities and flaws as soon as they appeared. The production team was able to rapidly address concerns and make process adjustments to prevent future errors since the real-time data analytics technology gave them relevant information. Consequently, the manufacturer attained a 20% decrease in defect rates and a significant improvement in the overall quality of the product, resulting in increased customer satisfaction and a decrease in return rates.

Case Study: Optimizing Supply Chain with Data-Driven Insights
An international food and beverage corporation had difficulties controlling its intricate supply chain, which included logistics, demand forecasting, and inventory control. The business put in place a complete data analytics system to streamline its supply chain processes. This solution gathered and examined information from multiple sources, including inventory levels, transportation logistics, and sales projections. The organization may manage inventory levels, forecast demand precisely, and expedite logistics operations by utilizing predictive analytics. As a result, the cost of keeping inventory was reduced by 15%, and on-time delivery improved by 10%. The company's capacity to react quickly to changes in the market was strengthened by the data-driven approach, which also increased supply chain efficiency overall.

1.7.3 Healthcare

Healthcare analytics is a specialist field that processes enormous amounts of historical and real-time data within the healthcare industry by using sophisticated analytical tools. Healthcare practitioners can have a thorough grasp of patient populations, treatment efficacy, and resource use by deriving insightful conclusions from this data. This method makes it easier to create tactics that are more focused and effective.

The main objective of healthcare analytics is to convert insights into practical actions that improve the standard of treatment. Healthcare analytics helps administrators and providers make evidence-based choices by spotting trends, patterns, and correlations. Enhancing patient outcomes, streamlining administrative procedures, and allocating resources optimally guarantee efficiency and cost-effectiveness in healthcare institutions.

Furthermore, using data-driven insights to tailor treatment plans and preventive care measures, healthcare analytics aims to improve the patient experience. In addition to improving health outcomes, this patient-centric approach makes the experience of navigating the healthcare system more enjoyable and fulfilling for people. In the end, healthcare analytics revolutionizes the provision of healthcare services, stimulates innovation, and promotes continual improvement. Although they have different goals, healthcare data analytics and health informatics work together to improve healthcare delivery. Healthcare data analytics, according to the American Health Information Management Association (AHIMA), is carefully analyzing data to find patterns and insights that support clinical decision-making and illness prevention. A larger field called health informatics combines people, procedures, and technology to enhance medical care. It entails developing systems to efficiently manage healthcare data and utilizing information technology to enhance healthcare decision-making and procedures. In the data-driven healthcare environment, these areas work together to spur innovation and enhance patient care.

Case Study: Predicting Patient Deterioration with Real-Time Analytics

Hospitals frequently face the issue of recognizing patients who are at danger of rapid health deterioration, which can result in delayed interventions and poor results. To solve this issue, a large healthcare provider created a real-time analytics platform that combines patient data from EHRs, vital sign monitors, and test findings. The system uses machine learning algorithms to anticipate which patients are likely to face critical health difficulties in the following 24 hours. The predictive approach identified at-risk patients with high accuracy, allowing healthcare teams to intervene early. As a result, the hospital lowered the number of severe complications by 30%, decreased ICU hospitalizations by 20%, and improved overall patient outcomes.

Case Study: Enhancing Operational Efficiency with Workforce Analytics

A large hospital experienced considerable issues in optimizing staff schedules, which frequently resulted in either overstaffing or understaffing in various areas, affecting both expenses and patient care quality. To address this issue, the hospital used workforce analytics to analyze historical data on patient admissions, peak hours, and staff availability. Using predictive analytics, the system projected patient intake and modified staffing accordingly. The introduction of workforce analytics resulted in a 15% labor cost reduction and a 10% increase in patient satisfaction scores. Furthermore, the hospital saw fewer cases of burnout among employees as a result of more balanced workloads, which contributed to a healthier working atmosphere and higher-quality treatment.

Case Study: Streamlining Emergency Department Operations with Analytics

A large metropolitan hospital's emergency department (ED) suffered with high wait times and overcrowding, hurting patient satisfaction and care quality. To solve these difficulties, the hospital implemented an analytics platform that utilized both historical and real-time data to enhance patient flow in the ED. The system examined patterns in patient arrivals, treatment times, and discharge procedures to identify bottlenecks and streamline operations. By utilizing data analytics to control patient flow, the hospital lowered average wait times by 40% while increasing patient throughput by 25%. Patient satisfaction levels increased dramatically, and the ED was better prepared to handle peak times, demonstrating the transformative power of analytics on operational efficiency and patient care.

Applications of Analytics in Sports

Sports analytics is the application of data analysis tools to improve different elements of sport, including player performance, team strategies, injury prevention, and spectator engagement. The use of analytics in sports has increased substantially as big data technology and improved statistical methodologies have emerged.

Applying analytics in sports involves a systematic approach to ensure that the insights derived are actionable and beneficial to the team or organization. The process typically involves defining objectives, collecting data, preprocessing the data, conducting data analysis, interpreting the results, and monitoring the outcomes.

The first step in any analytics effort is to set clear targets. Sports analytics aims might vary greatly, but they typically involve improving player performance, optimizing team plans, lowering injuries, and increasing spectator engagement. These objectives should be specified, measurable, attainable, relevant, and time-bound (SMART). A team may seek to improve shooting accuracy by 5% or reduce injuries through improved training practices. Aligning these objectives with the team's overarching strategy ensures that the analytics project contributes to larger corporate goals.

Once the objectives have been established, the following stage is to discover and collect relevant data from a variety of sources. In sports, data might come from game statistics, wearable gadgets, video analysis, and external elements like weather and travel itineraries. Game statistics track player performance, game outcomes, and other in-game metrics. Wearable gadgets, such as fitness trackers, track players' health and performance metrics, like heart rate and fatigue levels. Video analysis can help you grasp player movements, methods, and strategies. External data, such as weather and travel schedules, might have an impact on player performance and should be considered.

After data collection, it must be cleaned and preprocessed to ensure that it is ready for analysis. This stage entails addressing missing values, standardizing data, and converting it to a consistent format. Data preparation is critical to assuring the correctness and dependability of the study. Missing data, for example, can be managed using interpolation or the elimination of partial records, and differing data scales can be normalized to allow for meaningful comparisons.

To generate insights from clean data, proper analytical approaches are used. This can include descriptive analytics to summarize historical data, predictive analytics to forecast future outcomes, and prescriptive analytics to make recommendations for better decision-making. Descriptive analytics helps us understand the past by summarizing performance measures. Predictive analytics employs statistical models and machine learning approaches to forecast future events based on past data. Prescriptive analytics goes a step further by recommending activities to attain desired results based on predictive models.

The findings of the investigation are subsequently analyzed and transformed into actionable insights. This stage entails presenting the findings to coaches, players, and other stakeholders in an intelligible manner. For example, if the data shows that shooting accuracy improves when players are less exhausted, solutions could include specialized training programs to maintain ideal physical conditions or changes in shot selection strategies based on high-probability shot placements.

Finally, the outcomes of analytics-driven actions are regularly monitored and analyzed. This entails tracking performance data to assess the effectiveness of established tactics and making any necessary changes. This iterative method guarantees that analytics solutions are relevant and effective over time, allowing teams to constantly adapt their approaches and achieve their goals.

1.8   Predictive Analytics Tools

Several tools and software platforms are available to aid predictive analytics, each with a variety of features for data pretreatment, model construction, validation, and deployment. Here are some of the primary tools often utilized in predictive analytics.

1.8.1   Tableau

Tableau, created in 2003 by Christian Chabot, Pat Hanrahan, and Chris Stolte, is an advanced analytics platform that empowers users and companies by changing the way data is used to solve issues. This complete data and analytics system provides fully integrated data management and governance, allowing users to maintain control and ensure data is used responsibly. Tableau's visual analytics and data storytelling capabilities help users gain a better grasp of data insights. Salesforce's Einstein AI integration enhances cooperation by enabling for more intelligent and informed decision-making. Tableau Pulse offers tailored and accessible data experiences, making data more engaging to users of all levels of visualization competence.

Furthermore, Tableau Cloud provides a hosted, enterprise-grade analytics solution that enables smarter, insight-driven decisions through quick, flexible, and intuitive analytics. Tableau Prep Builder modernizes the data preparation process, making it faster and easier to integrate, shape, and clean data before analysis.

1.8.2   Amazon QuickSight

Amazon QuickSight is a cloud-based, unified business intelligence (BI) service created by Amazon Web Services. It is intended to provide scalable analytics solutions that empower consumers and businesses by changing the way data is processed and visualized. QuickSight enables customers to generate modern interactive dashboards, paginated reports, natural language queries, and embedded analytics using a single source of truth. Amazon QuickSight's natural language processing component, Amazon Q, enables business analysts and users to create, discover, and share important insights in seconds, speeding the impact of data-driven decisions.

QuickSight connects smoothly with other AWS services, resulting in smooth data flow and increased operational efficiency. It is noted for its user-friendly interface and ability to efficiently manage massive datasets, making it a popular choice among many enterprises. Over 100,000 clients use QuickSight to transform data insights into actionable steps. QuickSight also provides bespoke analytics experiences, making data accessible and interesting for people with varying levels of technical expertise.

Furthermore, QuickSight's cloud-based architecture offers a customizable and enterprise-grade analytics solution, allowing for faster, more informed decision-making. QuickSight modernizes the analytics process by providing capabilities such as natural language queries and interactive dashboards, making it easier for users to interact with and extract insights from their data.

1.8.3   IBM Cognos Analytics

IBM Cognos Analytics acts as your trusted business copilot, aiming to improve your intelligence, agility, and confidence in data-driven decision-making. It gives every user – whether a data scientist, business analyst, or non-IT specialist – the capacity to do relevant analysis in line with organizational goals. By easing the path from basic to advanced analytics, users can use data for exploration, discovering new insights, comprehending results, and challenging established standards. With IBM Cognos Analytics, you can easily display, analyze, and distribute actionable information within your organization.

IBM Cognos Analytics is a versatile product that includes features for filtering and selecting relevant criteria, integrated tools for meeting business objectives, and a dedicated workspace for creating business reports. Users commonly praise its ability to build informative dashboards, its user-friendly design, seamless integration with numerous data sources, and the simplicity of dashboard capabilities for tracking important performance metrics. However, users have reported that the initial setup and customizing process can be time-consuming, necessitating large hardware resources, resulting in resource-intensive activities and revealing a lack of transparent privacy safeguards.

1.8.4   SAS Viya

SAS Viya is a powerful, cloud-native platform designed to handle modern data analytics challenges with efficiency and scalability. It enables organizations to extract actionable insights from their data using advanced analytics, artificial intelligence, and machine learning. With its seamless integration across environments, SAS Viya ensures that data scientists, analysts, and business users can collaborate effectively to drive informed decision-making.

Summary

This chapter provided a comprehensive introduction to analytics, starting with an overview of its importance and the need for predictive analytics. We discussed game-changing innovations and different types of analytics, emphasizing their role in modern decision-making. Predictive analytics was explored in depth, including techniques for predicting binary outcomes and the use of various models such as decision trees. The chapter covered data sources and collection methods, including the use of data lakes as a collection platform. Additionally, we examined case studies across finance, manufacturing, and healthcare to highlight real-world applications of analytics. Tools for predictive analytics, such as Tableau, Amazon QuickSight, IBM Cognos Analytics, and SAS Viya, were reviewed. The chapter concluded with a summary and a lab experiment to reinforce the concepts discussed.

1.9   Lab Experiment

Aim: To perform analysis on a given dataset using SAS programming

Description
SAS programming is a flexible language for statistical analysis, data management, and visualization. It simplifies data manipulation, including importing, cleaning, and merging databases. SAS provides various statistical processes for descriptive and inferential analysis, including regression, ANOVA, and clustering. It provides customizable graphs and charts for data analysis and display. SAS allows you to efficiently manage massive datasets by subsetting, sorting, and filtering data. It allows for the generation of detailed reports summarizing analytical results for successful communication. SAS programming automates repetitious procedures, leading to more efficient and consistent analysis.

Input Data/Dataset: All the relevant data obtained for the experiment need to be included in this section. The data should be mentioned clearly with the help of a tabular structure and data units.

Data Analysis Steps

Importing Data

Imagine you have a list of information about students applying for jobs, like their grades and test scores. The first step is to bring this information into our analysis tool.

Printing Data

Once we have the data in our tool, we take a quick look at the first few students' IDs to make sure everything loaded correctly.

Computing Means

Next, we calculate the average grade (CGPA) among all the students. This gives us an idea of how the students are performing academically on average.

Descriptive Statistics

We then dig deeper into the grades by looking at statistics like the highest and lowest grades, as well as how spread out the grades are. This helps us understand the overall distribution of grades.

Frequency Analysis

We analyze how often different grades occur. For example, we might find out how many students have a particular grade point average (CGPA).

Printing Filtered Data (Placed Students)

Now, we focus on students who have been placed in jobs. We look at students who scored well on a test (AptitudeTestScore) and see if they got a job.

Printing Filtered Data (No Internships)

Similarly, we look at students who got jobs but didn't do any internships to understand if internships are necessary for job placement.

Data Manipulation

Finally, we start organizing the data in a way that's easier to understand. We create a new dataset with only the most important information about each student, like their ID, grades, and whether they received training for job placement. We also calculate a new value called "ratio," which compares a student's grades to the number of projects they've worked on.

> In simple terms, we're essentially taking a big list of student information, analyzing it to understand how well students are doing academically and in finding jobs, and then organizing the important bits into a neat summary.

Technology Stack Used: SAS Programming (SAS Studio)

```
 1  /* Importing the CSV file */
 2  proc import datafile="/Files/u63762121/sasuser.v94/placement.
      csv"
 3      out=work.placement
 4      dbms=csv
 5      replace;
 6  run;
 7
 8  /* Printing the first 10 observations with StudentID */
 9  proc print data=work.placement(obs=10);
10      var StudentID;
11  run;
12
13  /* Computing the mean of CGPA */
14  proc means data=work.placement;
15      var CGPA;
16  run;
17
18  /* Generating univariate statistics for CGPA */
19  proc univariate data=work.placement;
20      var CGPA;
21  run;
22
23  /* Frequency analysis of CGPA */
24  proc freq data=work.placement;
25      tables CGPA;
26  run;
27
28  /* Printing data for students placed with an
        AptitudeTestScore of 60 or higher */
29  proc print data=work.placement;
30      var PlacementStatus AptitudeTestScore StudentID;
31      where PlacementStatus="Placed" and AptitudeTestScore >=
        60;
32  run;
33
34  /* Printing data for students placed without any internships
        */
35  proc print data=work.placement;
36      var PlacementStatus Internships StudentID;
37      where PlacementStatus="Placed" and Internships = 0;
38  run;
39
40  /* Creating a new dataset myclass and copying placement data
        */
41  data myclass;
42      set work.placement;
43  run;
44
45  /* Keeping only the necessary columns and dropping others */
46  data myclass;
```

```
47      set work.placement;
48      keep StudentID CGPA PlacementTraining;
49      drop Internships Projects;
50 run;
51
52 /* Formatting CGPA to 1 decimal place */
53 data myclass;
54      set work.placement;
55      format CGPA 1.;
56 run;
57
58 /* Creating a new variable ratio which is CGPA divided by
       Projects */
59 data myclass;
60      set work.placement;
61      ratio = CGPA / Projects;
62 run;
63
64 /* Converting PlacementStatus to uppercase and keeping
       necessary columns */
65 data myclass;
66      set work.placement;
67      Type = upcase(PlacementStatus);
68      keep StudentID CGPA PlacementTraining PlacementStatus;
69 run;
```

Multiple Choice Questions

1. What is the primary purpose of analytics?
   a. To confuse data scientists
   b. To predict the future
   c. To create random graphs
   d. To make data disappear
2. Which section of analytics focuses on predicting future outcomes?
   a. Analytics Overview
   b. Why Analytics
   c. Predictive Analytics
   d. Predicting
3. What is one of the reasons why we need analytics?
   a. To increase confusion
   b. To make data irrelevant
   c. To make informed decisions
   d. To create chaos
4. Which tool is not mentioned as a predictive analytics tool?
   a. Tableau
   b. Amazon QuickSight
   c. IBM Cognos Analytics
   d. Excel

5. What is the focus of predictive analytics?
   a. Analyzing past data
   b. Predicting future outcomes
   c. Presenting current trends
   d. Ignoring data
6. In predictive analytics, what is used to predict binary outcomes?
   a. Random guesswork
   b. Advanced algorithms
   c. Excel formulas
   d. Tea leaves
7. Which section provides examples of predictive analytics?
   a. Why Analytics
   b. Types of Analytics
   c. Predicting
   d. Case Studies and Expert Opinion on Analytics
8. Which tool is described as a cloud-based analytics software suite?
   a. Tableau
   b. Amazon QuickSight
   c. IBM Cognos Analytics
   d. SAS Viya
9. Which industry is not mentioned in the case studies and expert opinions on analytics?
   a. Finance
   b. Manufacturing
   c. Healthcare
   d. Retail
10. Which type of predictive model is mentioned in the content?
    a. Neural networks
    b. Linear regression
    c. Decision trees
    d. All of the above

Long Answer Questions

1. Explain the importance of predictive analytics in modern business operations. Provide examples to support your answer.
2. Discuss the potential challenges organizations might face when implementing predictive analytics solutions. How can these challenges be overcome?
3. Compare and contrast the features of Tableau, Amazon QuickSight, and IBM Cognos Analytics as predictive analytics tools. Highlight their strengths and weaknesses.
4. Analyze the impact of predictive analytics on different industries such as finance, manufacturing, and healthcare. Provide real-world case studies or examples to illustrate your points.

5. Describe the process of building a predictive model using decision trees. Explain the steps involved and discuss some common pitfalls to avoid during model development.

Solution to MCQs

1. To predict the future
2. Predictive Analytics
3. To make informed decisions
4. Excel
5. Predicting future outcomes
6. Advanced algorithms
7. Predicting
8. Amazon QuickSight
9. Retail
10. Decision trees

Simple Linear Regression

2

Regression Analysis

Types of Regression, Simple Linear Regression (SLR), SLR Model Evaluation, SLR Estimation and Prediction, SLR Model Assumptions, Standard Error of Estimate, T-test, Categorical Predictors, Data Transformations, Model Building, Influential Points, Demonstration: R-Studio, Demonstration: SAS

2.1   Regression

Linear regression is a basic yet effective statistical method for determining the relationship between two variables. Assume you're trying to determine out how your study time influences your exam results. If you plot your study hours on a graph and compare them to your exam scores, you might see a pattern. Linear regression allows you to draw a straight line through this data, indicating the overall direction of the association. If the line moves upward, it indicates that greater study time is often correlated with higher grades. This line, known as the "regression line," predicts your exam result based on how many hours you study.

The beauty of linear regression rests in its simplicity and clarity. It not only indicates the direction of the relationship (positive or negative), but it also aids in quantification. For example, if the line is steep, it means that modest changes in study time result in substantial differences in scores. In contrast, a flatter line indicates that study time has a smaller impact on scores. While real-world data can be chaotic and does not always fit precisely along a straight line, linear regression offers a simple technique to make sense of and anticipate outcomes based on the information available.

© Ramchandra S Mangrulkar and Pallavi Vijay Chavan 2025
R. S. Mangrulkar and P. Vijay Chavan, *Predictive Analytics with SAS and R*,
https://doi.org/10.1007/979-8-8688-0905-7_2

2.2   Regression Analysis

One method for looking at one or more independent variables and one or more dependent variables is regression analysis. Data from many areas, including psychology, economics, finance, and the natural sciences, are routinely analyzed and modeled using it.

Regression analysis often begins with the development of a hypothesis or a theoretical understanding of how the variables of interest may be related. This initial conceptualization informs the selection of variables to include in the analysis as well as the shape of the regression model. For example, while researching the factors influencing house prices, researchers may hypothesize that variables such as location, square footage, and neighborhood demographics influence housing values.

Beyond prediction, regression analysis makes hypothesis testing and inference easier, allowing researchers to draw conclusions about the correlations between variables and the generalizability of findings to larger populations or situations. This inferential component is critical for making evidence-based decisions and drawing meaningful conclusions from data.

2.3   Types of Regression

There are several types of regression:

Simple linear regression: The most basic kind of regression has just one predicted variable and one predictor variable, and it is called simple linear regression. Variables in the regression equation are supposed to have a linear relationship: x is the predictor variable, y is the variable to be predicted on the basis x, the line's intercept is b, and its slope is m.

Multiple linear regression: This statistical technique, known as multiple linear regression, is employed by analysts to assess the variance of the model and determine the relative contributions of each independent variable to the overall variance. By incorporating two or more independent variables, this method forecasts the value of a dependent variable.

Logistic regression: When there are two possible outcomes for the dependent variable, logistic regression is utilized instead of linear regression. It simulates the likelihood that the dependent variable will fall into a specific group. Any real integer can be mapped to a probability value between zero and one using the logistic function.

2.3.1   Simple Linear Regression (SLR)

SLR seeks to identify a linear connection between an independent and a potentially dependent variable in order to characterize the relationship between them. Using a regression line, the method known as interpolation may be used to estimate or predict missing data.

A simple linear regression model consists of one independent variable and one dependent variable. By determining the slope as well as the intercept of the best fit line, the model illustrates the connections between the variables.

When the predictor variable is zero, the intercept shows the predicted variable's anticipated value; when the predictor variable varies for each unit, the slope shows this variation.

Figure 2-1 shows the linear relationship between the predicted variable (X) and output (Y) variables. The blue line is the most appropriate straight line. Making a line that most nearly resembles the given data points is our aim.

2.3.2   SLR Model Evaluation

Evaluating a simple linear regression model entails determining the model's ability to suit the data and how precise predictions it makes. The following are some typical techniques for assessing a basic linear regression model:

Coefficient of determination (R-squared): The R-squared calculation displays the percentage of the dependent variable's variance that can be predicted using the independent variable. It ranges from zero to one, with one indicating the best match.

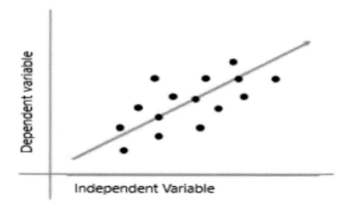

Figure 2-1. Linear relationship between X and Y

R-squared, however, may not provide a clear picture of the model's efficacy on its own. The formula for calculating the R-squared error is

$$R^2 = 1 - \frac{\sum_{i=1}^{n}(y_i - \hat{y}_i)^2}{\sum_{i=1}^{n}(y_i - \bar{y})^2} \tag{2-1}$$

where

y_i : Actual values

$\hat{y}_i$: Predicted values

$\bar{y}$: Mean of the actual values

n : Number of observations

Residual analysis: Residual plots can demonstrate if the residuals are randomly distributed around zero, indicating that the linear regression assumptions are met. Residual patterns indicate that the model may lack critical variables or that the relationship is not linear.

Figure 2-2 represents the plot for actual and predicted values and the formula to calculate the residual.

Mean squared error (MSE): MSE is the average square difference (also known as the difference between observed and predicted values). The error is expressed in the same units as the dependent variable using RMSE, which is the square root of MSE. Lower numbers indicate improved model performance.

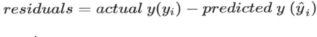

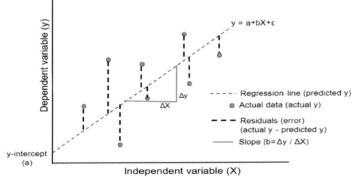

Figure 2-2. Residual analysis

The formula for calculating the mean squared error (MSE) is

$$\text{MSE} = \frac{1}{n} \sum_{i=1}^{n} (y_i - \hat{y}_i)^2 \tag{2-2}$$

where

y_i : Actual values

$\hat{y}_i$: Predicted values

n : Number of observations

Mean absolute error (MAE): MAE represents the average absolute difference between observed and anticipated values. Lower values, such as MSE and RMSE, imply improved model performance.

The formula for calculating the mean absolute error (MAE) is

$$\text{MAE} = \frac{1}{n} \sum_{i=1}^{n} \left| y_i - \hat{y}_i \right| \tag{2-3}$$

where

y_i : Actual values

$\hat{y}_i$: Predicted values

n : Number of observations

Coefficient of correlation: Pearson's coefficient r, which also indicates the intensity and direction of the connection, reveals that the two types of variables have a linear relationship. It ranges from one to one, with one representing a perfect positive linear relationship, one representing a perfect negative linear relationship, and zero indicating no linear relationship.

The formula for calculating Pearson's correlation coefficient r is

$$r = \frac{n \sum_{i=1}^{n} x_i y_i - \sum_{i=1}^{n} x_i \sum_{i=1}^{n} y_i}{\sqrt{\left(n \sum_{i=1}^{n} x_i^2 - \left(\sum_{i=1}^{n} x_i \right)^2 \right) \left(n \sum_{i=1}^{n} y_i^2 - \left(\sum_{i=1}^{n} y_i \right)^2 \right)}} \tag{2-4}$$

where

$$x_i : \text{Values of the first variable}$$
$$y_i : \text{Values of the second variable}$$
$$n : \text{Number of observations}$$

2.3.3   SLR Estimation and Prediction

The following steps are implemented to perform simple linear regression for estimation and prediction:

Step 1 – Data collection: Collect a dataset consisting of pairs of observations for the independent variable (X) and the dependent variable (Y).

Step 2 – Data exploration: Explore the data visually using scatter plots and summary statistics to understand the relationship between the variables.

Step 3 – Model selection: Assess whether there is a linear relationship between the variables based on the data exploration. If yes, use basic linear regression to continue.

Step 4 – Model estimation: Calculate the linear regression model's parameters The model equation is usually shown:

$$Y = \beta_0 + \beta_1 X + \varepsilon$$

whereas the expected variable is denoted by Y.

The predictor variable is X.
The y-intercept is β_0.
The slope coefficient, or regression coefficient, is β_1.
The error term is ε.

The coefficients β_0 and β_1 are estimated using least squares regression.

Step 5 – Prediction: The model may be used to make predictions after it has been fitted and evaluated. To anticipate the value of the predicted variable (Y), add a new value to the predictor variable (X) in the regression equation:
Y = a+bX where Y is the predicted value of the predicted variable and a and b are the estimated coefficients from the regression model.

Real-World Example

1. We collect data on house prices and sizes.
2. We explore the data and see a linear relationship between price and size of the house.
3. We fit a simple linear regression model: Price $= \beta_0 + \beta_1 \times$ Size $+ \varepsilon$.
4. We estimate the coefficients β_0 and β_1 using least squares regression.
5. We assess the models goodness-of-fit using metrics like R-squared.
6. Finally, we can make predictions for new house sizes using the fitted model.

2.3.4 Applications of SLR

Economics: Variables like income and expenditure, price and quantity sold, and supply and demand can all be studied using simple linear regression.

Finance: In finance, simple linear regression can be used to study how various factors, such as interest rates and inflation, stock prices and trading volume, or GDP growth and unemployment rates, relate to each other.

Promoting: Advertising expenditure on sales, pricing strategies, and customer demand can be studied with simple linear regression.

Health: When it comes to healthcare, simple linear regression can be used to investigate how various factors, such as patient age and blood pressure, dosage and drug effectiveness, or income and healthcare expenditure, interact with one another.

Education: Simple linear regression can be applied to study the relationship between variables like study time and exam scores, class size and academic performance, or teacher experience and student achievement.

Quality control: Simple linear regression can help analyze the relationship between variables such as manufacturing process parameters and product quality, input parameters and output characteristics, or time and defect rates.

Predictive modeling: Simple linear regression can be used as a building block in more complex predictive models, providing insights into relationships that can be useful for forecasting or decision-making.

2.4   Demonstration of SLR Using Python

```
import numpy as np
from sklearn.linear_model import LinearRegression
import matplotlib.pyplot as plt

# Feature matrix
X = np.array([2, 1, 3, 5, 4]).reshape(-1, 1)

# Target vector
y = np.array([3, 2, 5, 4, 6])

# Create a linear regression model
model = LinearRegression()

# Fit the model to the data
model.fit(X, y)

# Make predictions
y_pred = model.predict(X)

# Print the coefficients
print('Intercept:', model.intercept_)
print('Slope:', model.coef_[0])

# Plot the data and the fitted line
plt.scatter(X, y, color='red')
plt.plot(X, y_pred, color='blue')
plt.xlabel('X')
plt.ylabel('y')
plt.title('Simple Linear Regression')
plt.show()
```

The output of the code is given in Figure 2-3.

2.5   T-test

This section introduces the idea of the t-test which is a basic statistical method for comparing the means of two groups. In order to check whether there is a significant difference in means and, consequently, derive relevant inferences from our data, the t-test is an indispensable tool in research.

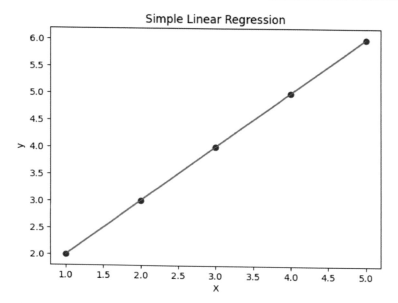

Figure 2-3. Plot for simple linear regression using Python

Table 2-1. Example Dataset
1 for Independent Samples
T-test

Student ID	Exam Score	Group
1	85	A
2	78	A
3	92	A
4	80	B
5	87	B
6	94	B

2.5.1   Types of T-tests

There are *two* main types of t-tests:

1. **Independent samples t-test:** The independent samples t-test is used to compare the means of two different groups. With the help of this test, we can find out, for example, whether the exam results of students who attended online courses and traditional lectures differ. Table 2-1 shows a dataset containing exam scores of two groups of students: Group A (traditional lecture-based) and Group B (online course-based). The variables are Student ID, Exam Score, and Group (A or B).

   Using Example Dataset 1, we will create histograms depicting the distribution of exam scores for Group A and Group B as shown in Figure 2-4.

   We will also construct box plots to compare the exam score distributions between Group A and Group B as given in Figure 2-5.

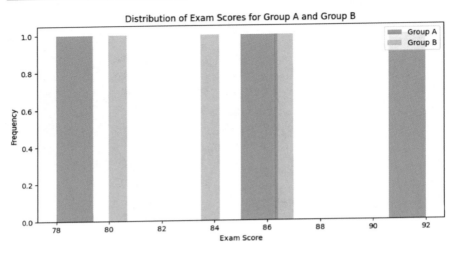

Figure 2-4. Distribution of exam scores for Group A and Group B

2. **Paired-samples t-test:** The paired-samples t-test is another topic that is useful when looking at related groups. For example, you can test whether test scores improve significantly before and after students use a particular teaching strategy. Table 2-2 shows a dataset containing exam scores of students before and after undergoing a teaching intervention. The variables are Student ID, Pre-test Score, and Post-test Score. Using Example Dataset 2, a line graph will illustrate the mean exam scores before and after the teaching intervention, aiding in visualizing any changes over time as shown in Figure 2-6.

2.6   Categorical Predictors

In simple linear regression, the focus is typically on modeling the relationship between a single continuous independent variable (predictor) and a single continuous dependent variable (response). However, it's also possible to include categorical predictors in simple linear regression using a technique called "dummy coding" or "indicator coding."

1. **Dummy coding:** Suppose you have a categorical predictor with two levels (e.g., "male" and "female"). You can create a dummy variable that takes the value of 1 for one level and 0 for the other level. For example, you might create a dummy variable X_1 where $X_1 = 1$ for males and $X_1 = 0$ for females.
2. **Extension to multiple levels:** If you have a categorical predictor with more than two levels (e.g., "red," "blue," and "green"), you can create multiple dummy variables. For example, if you have three levels, you would create two dummy

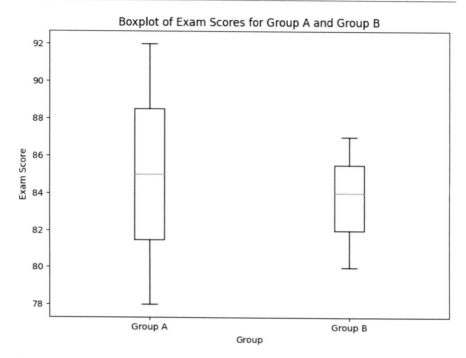

Figure 2-5. Box plot of exam scores for Group A and Group B

Table 2-2. Example Dataset
2 for Paired-Samples T-test

Student ID	Exam Score	Group
1	60	65
2	75	78
3	80	85
4	70	72
5	85	88
6	78	82

variables. One dummy variable would indicate whether the observation belongs to level 1 (e.g., $X_1 = 1$ for "red" and 0 otherwise), and the other dummy variable would indicate whether the observation belongs to level 2 (e.g., $X_2 = 1$ for "blue" and 0 otherwise). The remaining level would serve as the reference category.

3. **Model specification:** Once you've created dummy variables for the categorical predictor, you can include them in the simple linear regression model alongside the continuous predictor(s). The model would then take the form

$$Y = \beta_0 + \beta_1 X_{\text{continuous}} + \beta_2 X_1 + \beta_3 X_2 + \ldots + e$$

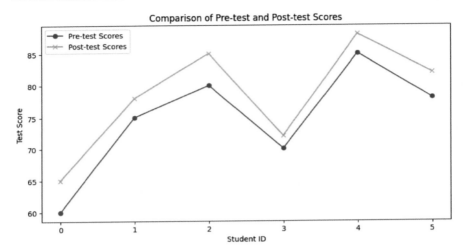

Figure 2-6. Comparison of Pre-test and Post-test Scores

where Y is the predicted variable, $X_{continuous}$ is the continuous predictor, and $X_1, X_2, \ldots$ are the dummy variables representing the categorical predictor.

2.6.1   Unveiling Categorical Predictors

Traits or ratings are represented by categorical predictors. These are not numeric variables; rather, they record qualitative data, for example, blood types (A, B, AB, O), car models (Toyota Camry, Honda Accord, Ford F-150), and hair colors (blonde, brown, black). The categorical forecast levels each represent a different category.

2.6.2   Nominal vs. Ordinal Categorical Predictors

Nominal predictors are categories that have no natural order. Nominal examples are blood type, car model, and hair color. Although sequence projections have an inherent order, levels are not always equally spaced. An example of a typical customer satisfaction rating is very unhappy, dissatisfied, neutral, satisfied, and very satisfied.

2.6.3   The Power of Prediction

Regression analysis: They can be incorporated into models to explain variance in a continuous response variable using methods such as effect coding or dummy coding.

Classification: For many classification problems, the target variables are categorical predictors. For example, using text features to predict whether we have spam or not.

2.6.4   Data Visualization

Investigating correlations between categorical predictors and other variables is made possible by data visualization:

Bar charts: Analyze means or frequencies among many categories

Box plots: Show how a continuous response variable is distributed over several categories

Pie charts: Show how a nominal categorical variable is proportionately composed

A deeper understanding of data activities is possible using categorical predictors. Important insights and intelligent decisions can be made by integrating them with statistical models and using perceptive data visualization methods.

2.7   Data Transformations

This section discusses important concepts that guide data transformations, which are central aspects of data analysis. It explores the theoretical foundations and statistical principles of data transformation and highlights the considerations and factors to consider in choosing the most appropriate transformations to prepare data for accurate analysis and modeling.

Data transformations are more than just aesthetic changes; they are based on statistical theory and created to solve certain problems with data analysis. Here is a closer examination of the theoretical ideas:

Central Limit Theorem (CLT):   Central Limit Theory (CLT) is a fundamental theory of statistics, according to which the sum of a sufficient number of independent random variables, regardless of their initial distribution, tends under certain conditions to a normal distribution (bell curve). Transformations commonly provided in statistical tests and modeling strategies, such as linear regression, can be used to move data toward normality.

Homoscedasticity: The assumption of equal variance for groups or levels of multiple factors in statistical models is called homoscedasticity. Homoscedasticity can be achieved through transformations, which increases the validity of statistical inferences.

Linearity: Many statistical models, including linear regression, assume a linear relationship between the independent and dependent variables. A more linear relationship can be created with transformations, which improves the accuracy of model interpretations and predictions.

2.7.1   Choosing the Right Tool

The data itself, the analytic objectives, and the underlying theoretical presumptions of the intended statistical methods must all be carefully taken into account when choosing the best data transformation. Here are some important things to think about:

Data distribution: It is important to understand the distribution of the output data, such as skewed or normal. Skewed distributions can be manipulated and brought closer to normal using transformations such as logarithmic or square root transformations.

Statistical assumptions: Necessary transformations are determined by special statistical tests or models created for the analysis. Reviewing the theoretical basis of these techniques will help select appropriate modifications to ensure accurate and reliable results.

2.7.2   Beyond Normality

While returning the data to its original state is frequently the aim of data transformation, it is not always the only one. Different theoretical frameworks may be used, depending on the objectives of the analysis and the statistical techniques selected:

Non-parametric statistics: These techniques may use little or no data transformations and assume fewer underlying data distributions.

Machine learning algorithms: Many machine learning algorithms may not require significant data transformations because they tolerate deviations from normality. However, one of the most important factors in improving model performance is often feature design, which may involve transformations.

2.8   Model Building

This chapter takes an in-depth look at a key component of data science: model development. It explores key ideas, different approaches, and factors to consider when building reliable models to gain insight from data.

2.8.1 Facets of Model Building

The process of constructing a mathematical representation of a link between features in input data and a target variable in the desired output is known as model building. Once trained on previous data, these models can be used to forecast upcoming occurrences or yet-to-be-discovered data points. The following are important facets of model building:

Predictive power: Enabling accurate predictions is the main goal of model building. A well-designed model should ideally be able to generalize well, which means it should perform well on new data that is not from the training set.

Data-driven approach: Using models, data can be analyzed to find trends and relationships, allowing data to be derived and turned into useful insights using this data strategy.

Types of models: There are many different methods of model creation available, and each has its advantages and disadvantages. The specific problem you are trying to solve and the characteristics of your data will determine which model is best for you.

2.8.2 Common Model Building Techniques

A wide range of strategies are available in the field of model development, each specifically designed to tackle distinct prediction issues. Here's a peek at a few widely used approaches:

Linear regression: An important method for simulating a continuous interaction between one or more independent variables and a dependent variable. It is good enough to find linear correlations in data.

Classification: Classification models aim to predict categorical outcomes, for example, to determine whether we have spam or not or to predict customer churn (probability that a user will stop the service). Methods such as logistic regression, decision trees, and support vector machines (SVM) are commonly used in classification tasks.

Regression trees: These tree-based models create a decision tree that leads to a predicted outcome by segmenting the data according to characteristics. Because they are interpretable, it is easier to understand the reasoning behind the model's predictions.

Ensemble methods: Using ensemble approaches, multiple models are combined to produce a more reliable and accurate model. Ensemble methods include gradient boosting and random forests.

Deep learning: The architecture and functioning of the human brain is the inspiration for deep learning models, a branch of machine learning. They can be very powerful tools for tasks like image recognition and natural language processing and can thrive in handling complex multidimensional data.

2.8.3   Crafting a Model

Data preparation: Every good model starts with quality data. Important tasks in data processing are data cleaning, correction of missing data, and feature engineering (making new features out of old ones).

Model selection: Choosing the right model for a given problem is crucial. Consider the nature of the target variable (continuous vs. categorical), the characteristics of the data, and the interpretability required.

Model training and evaluation: A second holding set (the test set) is used to evaluate the models after they have been trained on a subset of the data (the training set). Model performance is evaluated using evaluation metrics such as precision, accuracy, recall, and F1 scores.

Model tuning: Hyperparameter tuning is the process of fine-tuning model parameters to increase performance. Methods such as random search or grid search can be used for this.

Model interpretation: It is important to understand how the model makes its predictions, especially when making important judgments. Techniques such as feature significance analysis can be useful for interpreting model behavior.

2.9   Influential Points

Influential points, also called leverage points or outliers, have an extraordinary ability to significantly influence the results of statistical models and studies. Identifying influential points is important because they have the ability to dramatically change regression lines, means, and other statistical indicators, which in turn affect the interpretation of data and drawing conclusions.

2.9.1   Key Characteristics of Influential Points

1. **Outliers:** In a dataset, influential points usually appear as outliers, far from most of the data points. These biases can distort the underlying trends in the data and distort the statistical analysis.
2. **High gain:** One characteristic that distinguishes influential points is their high gain, indicating that they have the ability to significantly change the parameters of regression models. These points often draw the regression line disproportionately, causing the slope and intercept to change significantly.
3. **Impact on results:** Estimates of statistical variables such as means, variances, and correlation coefficients may be biased when significant scores are present. Ignoring these factors can lead to incorrect conclusions and errors in data interpretation.
4. **Identification methods:** There are several statistical methods for finding significant points in a dataset. These are metrics that help identify data points that have

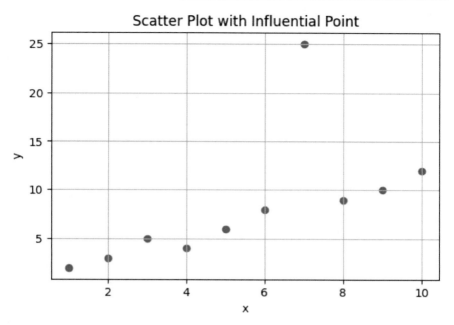

Figure 2-7. Scatter plot with influential point

a large impact on the results of statistical analyses, such as leverage statistics, explored residuals, and Cook's distance.

Let's create a simple dataset with an influential point and generate a scatter plot to illustrate its impact. This dataset contains x and y values, with an influential point (7, 25) where the y-value is significantly higher compared to other data points.

Figure 2-7 illustrates the relationship between the x and y variables from the example example dataset given in Table 2-3. Each data point is represented by a marker on the plot. The presence of an influential point (7, 25) is evident, as it deviates markedly from the general trend observed among the other data points.

2.9.2   Ridge and Lasso Regression

Ridge and Lasso regression are two effective strategies for addressing multi-collinearity and improving the predictive accuracy of regression models, especially when dealing with polynomial terms and nonlinear interactions. Both methods incorporate regularization into the regression model, which aids in controlling overfitting and increasing model generalization.

Table 2-3. Example Dataset
3 with Influential Point

x	y
1	2
2	3
3	5
4	4
5	6
6	8
7	25
8	9
9	10
10	12

Ridge Regression

Ridge regression, also known as Tikhonov regularization, penalizes the loss function by the square of the coefficient magnitude. This penalty term, commonly known as the L2 norm, discourages large coefficients and aids in managing multicollinearity. The ridge regression objective function can be expressed as

$$\min_{\beta} \left\{ \sum_{i=1}^{n}(y_i - \beta_0 - \sum_{j=1}^{p} \beta_j x_{ij})^2 + \lambda \sum_{j=1}^{p} \beta_j^2 \right\} \qquad (2\text{-}5)$$

The regularization parameter λ determines the penalty's intensity. A higher λ value reduces coefficients more, resulting in simpler models. Ridge regression is especially effective when working with polynomial terms since it reduces the possibility of overfitting caused by the inclusion of higher-degree polynomial features.

Example Suppose we have a dataset with a nonlinear relationship between the predictor x and the response variable y. By introducing polynomial terms (e.g., x^2, x^3), we can capture the nonlinear pattern. However, this also increases the risk of overfitting. By applying ridge regression with an appropriate λ, we can reduce the magnitudes of the polynomial coefficients, resulting in a more robust model that generalizes better to unseen data.

Lasso Regression

Lasso regression (Least Absolute Shrinkage and Selection Operator) penalizes the loss function by adding the absolute value of the coefficient magnitudes. This penalty component, known as the L1 norm, might reduce some coefficients to zero, so performing variable selection. The lasso regression's goal function is

$$\min_{\beta} \left\{ \sum_{i=1}^{n}(y_i - \beta_0 - \sum_{j=1}^{p} \beta_j x_{ij})^2 + \lambda \sum_{j=1}^{p} |\beta_j| \right\} \qquad (2\text{-}6)$$

Similar to ridge regression, λ determines the penalty strength. A greater λ causes more coefficients to shrink to zero, resulting in a simpler model with fewer predictors. Lasso regression is very useful when we suspect that many of the features, such as polynomial terms, are useless or redundant.

Example Consider the same dataset that includes polynomial terms. By using lasso regression, we may discover and keep only the most essential polynomial traits while reducing the coefficients of less important ones to zero. This not only helps to manage multicollinearity but also improves model interpretability by streamlining the feature set.

Ridge and Lasso regression are useful strategies for dealing with nonlinear relationships and polynomial terms in regression models. By combining these strategies, we may strike a compromise between model complexity and prediction performance, ensuring that the models generalize well to new data while capturing key trends in the data.

2.10 Survival Analysis Using the Cox Proportional Hazards Model

Survival analysis is a discipline of statistics that studies time-to-event data. It is used to estimate the time until an event of interest occurs, such as death, failure, or relapse. The Cox proportional hazards model, often known as the Cox regression model, is a popular survival analysis tool. This model is particularly effective for investigating the link between individuals' survival time and one or more predictor factors.

2.10.1 The Cox Proportional Hazards Model

The Cox proportional hazards model is a semi-parametric model that makes no assumptions about baseline hazard functions. Instead, it assumes that an individual's hazard function is a combination of a baseline hazard function and an exponential function of the predictor variables. The hazard function $h(t)$ for an individual with covariates x is given by

$$h(t|x) = h_0(t)\exp(\beta_1 x_1 + \beta_2 x_2 + \cdots + \beta_p x_p) \tag{2-7}$$

where

- $h(t|x)$ is the hazard function at time t given the covariates x.
- $h_0(t)$ is the baseline hazard function at time t.
- $\beta_1, \beta_2, \ldots, \beta_p$ are the coefficients corresponding to the covariates $x_1, x_2, \ldots, x_p$.

The key assumption of the Cox model is the proportional hazards assumption, which states that the ratio of the hazard functions for any two individuals is constant over time and is given by

$$\frac{h(t|x_1)}{h(t|x_2)} = \exp(\beta(x_1 - x_2)) \qquad (2\text{-}8)$$

2.10.2 Example of Cox Proportional Hazards Model

Consider a study of patients' survival times following a certain type of surgery. The goal is to establish how various factors, such as age, treatment kind, and health status, influence survival time. Assume we have the following covariates:

- x_1: Age of the patient
- x_2: Type of treatment (1 for Treatment A, 0 for Treatment B)
- x_3: Health condition (measured by a health score)

The Cox proportional hazards model can be specified as

$$h(t|x) = h_0(t) \exp(\beta_1 x_1 + \beta_2 x_2 + \beta_3 x_3) \qquad (2\text{-}9)$$

After fitting the model to the data, we might find the following estimated coefficients:

- $\hat{\beta}_1 = 0.02$
- $\hat{\beta}_2 = -0.5$
- $\hat{\beta}_3 = 0.1$

These coefficients represent the effect of each covariate on the hazard function. A coefficient of 0.02 for age indicates a small increase in risk with each additional year of age. The negative coefficient for treatment type indicates that Treatment A is associated with a lower hazard than Treatment B. Similarly, a positive correlation for the health condition score suggests that better health scores are related with greater risk.

2.10.3 Interpreting the Results

The Cox proportional hazards model calculates hazard ratios for each covariate, which represent the proportionate risk of the event occurring. For instance, if the hazard ratio for treatment type is $\exp(-0.5) \approx 0.61$, it suggests that patients receiving Treatment A have 39% reduced probability of the event occurring compared to those receiving Treatment B, keeping other parameters constant.

The Cox proportional hazards model is a versatile and effective survival analysis technique that allows researchers to investigate the effect of many factors on the time before an event. Because it does not assume a predefined baseline hazard function, it allows for greater flexibility when modeling complex interactions and is frequently used in medical research, engineering, and other industries that require time-to-event data.

Summary

This chapter provided an in-depth exploration of fundamental statistical methods and their applications. We began with a discussion on regression analysis and its various types, including simple linear regression (SLR), its evaluation, estimation, prediction, and practical applications. The chapter demonstrated SLR using Python, illustrating the method's implementation in a programming context. We then covered the t-test and its different types, followed by a focus on categorical predictors, distinguishing between nominal and ordinal types, and emphasizing their predictive power and visualization. Data transformations were examined, detailing the selection of appropriate methods and addressing issues beyond normality. The chapter further explored model building, including common techniques and the process of crafting a model. Influential points in regression were discussed, highlighting their key characteristics and the application of ridge and lasso regression for handling such points. Finally, we introduced survival analysis using the Cox proportional hazards model, including an example and guidance on interpreting results. The chapter concluded with a lab experiment to reinforce the theoretical concepts discussed.

2.11   Lab Experiment

The R script is intended for complete sports data analysis, which includes everything from data loading to advanced analysis. The process begins with loading important libraries (`dplyr`, `ggplot2`, `corrplot`, `caret`) and importing the dataset (`sports_data.csv`). An initial exploratory analysis is performed to review the dataset, which includes summary statistics and missing value checks.

The script then proceeds with data cleaning, converting categorical variables and handling missing values. A new variable, `Average_Points_Per_Game`, is added to enhance the dataset. Visualization tasks follow, including creating a histogram of points scored, a box plot comparing points across teams, and a correlation matrix of performance metrics, with results saved as PNG files.

In the predictive modeling section, the script splits the data into training and test sets, builds a linear regression model to predict points scored, and evaluates the model using root mean squared error (RMSE). It also includes optional k-means clustering to group players by performance metrics, with visualizations of the clustering results. The script offers a thorough approach to sports data analysis,

providing insights through exploration, visualization, prediction, and advanced
clustering.

```r
# sports_analysis.R

# Load necessary libraries
library(dplyr)
library(ggplot2)
library(corrplot)
library(caret)

# Load the dataset
sports_data <- read.csv("sports_data.csv")

# Explore the Data
print("First few rows of the dataset:")
print(head(sports_data))

print("Summary statistics:")
print(summary(sports_data))

print("Check for missing values:")
print(sapply(sports_data, function(x) sum(is.na(x))))

# Data Cleaning and Transformation
# Convert columns to appropriate data types if necessary
sports_data$Team <- as.factor(sports_data$Team)

# Handle missing values (if any)
sports_data <- na.omit(sports_data)

# Create new variables (e.g., average points per game)
sports_data <- sports_data %>%
  mutate(Average_Points_Per_Game = Points_Scored / Games_
    Played)

# Data Visualization

# Histogram of Points Scored
ggplot(sports_data, aes(x = Points_Scored)) +
  geom_histogram(binwidth = 10, fill = "blue", color = "black
    ") +
  labs(title = "Distribution of Points Scored", x = "Points
    Scored", y = "Frequency") +
  ggsave("points_scored_histogram.png")

# Boxplot of Points Scored by Team
ggplot(sports_data, aes(x = Team, y = Points_Scored, fill =
    Team)) +
  geom_boxplot() +
  labs(title = "Points Scored by Team", x = "Team", y = "
    Points Scored") +
  theme(axis.text.x = element_text(angle = 45, hjust = 1)) +
```

```r
46    ggsave("points_scored_boxplot.png")
47
48 # Correlation matrix of numerical variables
49 cor_data <- sports_data %>% select(Points_Scored, Assists,
      Rebounds, Average_Points_Per_Game)
50 cor_matrix <- cor(cor_data)
51 corrplot(cor_matrix, method = "circle")
52 ggsave("correlation_matrix.png")
53
54 # Predictive Modeling
55
56 # Split the data into training and test sets
57 set.seed(123) # For reproducibility
58 train_index <- createDataPartition(sports_data$Points_Scored,
      p = 0.8, list = FALSE)
59 train_data <- sports_data[train_index, ]
60 test_data <- sports_data[-train_index, ]
61
62 # Build a linear regression model
63 model <- lm(Points_Scored ~ Assists + Rebounds + Average_
      Points_Per_Game, data = train_data)
64
65 # Summarize the model
66 print("Linear Regression Model Summary:")
67 print(summary(model))
68
69 # Make predictions on the test set
70 predictions <- predict(model, newdata = test_data)
71
72 # Evaluate model performance
73 actuals <- test_data$Points_Scored
74 rmse <- sqrt(mean((predictions - actuals)^2))
75 cat("Root Mean Squared Error (RMSE):", rmse, "\n")
76
77 # Advanced Analysis (Optional)
78
79 # K-means clustering of players based on their performance
      metrics
80 # Prepare data for clustering
81 cluster_data <- sports_data %>% select(Points_Scored, Assists
      , Rebounds)
82 set.seed(123)
83 clusters <- kmeans(cluster_data, centers = 3)
84
85 # Add cluster assignments to the dataset
86 sports_data$Cluster <- as.factor(clusters$cluster)
87
88 # Visualize clusters
89 ggplot(sports_data, aes(x = Points_Scored, y = Assists, color
      = Cluster)) +
90   geom_point() +
91   labs(title = "Player Clustering", x = "Points Scored", y =
      "Assists") +
```

```
92    ggsave("player_clustering.png")
93
94 print("Analysis complete. Visualizations saved.")
```

Multiple Choice Questions

1. What is the primary purpose of simple linear regression?
   a. To model the relationship between two variables
   b. To analyze categorical data
   c. To perform clustering analysis
   d. To reduce the dimensionality of data
2. In the linear regression equation $Y = \beta_0 + \beta_1 X + \epsilon$, what does β_1 represent?
   a. The intercept
   b. The slope
   c. The error term
   d. The predicted value
3. What does the intercept β_0 indicate in a simple linear regression model?
   a. The change in Y for a unit change in X
   b. The value of Y when X is zero
   c. The error in the model
   d. The slope of the regression line
4. Which Python library is commonly used for fitting a linear regression model?
   a. Numpy
   b. Pandas
   c. Matplotlib
   d. Scikit-learn
5. In the context of simple linear regression, what is the purpose of the residual ϵ?
   a. To represent the slope of the line
   b. To measure the prediction accuracy
   c. To account for the difference between observed and predicted values
   d. To normalize the data
6. How do you interpret a high R-squared value in a simple linear regression model?
   a. The model explains a large portion of the variance in the dependent variable.
   b. The independent variable is not significant.
   c. The model is overfitting the data.
   d. The residuals are not normally distributed.
7. What is the primary assumption of simple linear regression?
   a. The relationship between the independent and dependent variables is quadratic.
   b. The relationship between the independent and dependent variables is linear.
   c. There is no relationship between the independent and dependent variables.
   d. The independent variable is categorical.

8. Which plot is commonly used to visualize the relationship in simple linear regression?
   a. Box plot
   b. Histogram
   c. Scatter plot
   d. Bar chart
9. What does a residual plot indicate in simple linear regression?
   a. The distribution of the independent variable
   b. The distribution of the dependent variable
   c. The difference between observed and predicted values
   d. The correlation between two variables
10. Which method is used to estimate the parameters of a simple linear regression model?
   a. Maximum likelihood estimation
   b. Gradient descent
   c. Ordinary least squares
   d. Support vector machines

Long Answer Questions

1. Explain the concept of simple linear regression and its assumptions. Discuss how it can be used to predict future outcomes.
2. Describe the process of fitting a simple linear regression model to a dataset. Include the steps of data collection, data exploration, model selection, and model estimation.
3. Discuss the interpretation of the slope and intercept in a simple linear regression model. Provide a real-world example to illustrate their significance.
4. Explain the role of the residual term in simple linear regression. How can residual analysis be used to evaluate the fit of the model?
5. Compare simple linear regression with multiple linear regression. Highlight the similarities and differences, and provide examples of when each method is appropriate to use.

Solution to MCQs

1. To model the relationship between two variables
2. The slope
3. The value of Y when X is zero
4. Scikit-learn
5. To account for the difference between observed and predicted values

6. The model explains a large portion of the variance in the dependent variable.
7. The relationship between the independent and dependent variables is linear.
8. Scatter plot
9. The difference between observed and predicted values
10. Ordinary least squares

Multiple Linear Regression

3

Multiple Linear Regression

Introduction to Multiple Linear Regression, Types of Regression, Model Building and Selection, Interpretation of Coefficients, Interaction Effects, Model Assumptions and Diagnostics, Multicollinearity, Standard Error of Estimate, T-test and F-test, Categorical Predictors, Data Transformations, Model Evaluation and Validation, Influential Points, Demonstration: R-Studio, Demonstration: SAS

3.1 Introduction to Multiple Regression

Within multiple regression, coefficients signify the association between each independent variable and the dependent variable. Each coefficient measures the alteration in the dependent variable linked with a one-unit change in the respective independent variable while maintaining all other variables constant.

$$Y = \beta_0 + \beta_1 X_1 + \beta_2 X_2 + \ldots + \beta_n X_n + \varepsilon$$

where

- Y is the dependent variable.
- $X_1, X_2, \ldots, X_n$ are the independent variables.
- $\beta_0, \beta_1, \ldots, \beta_n$ are the coefficients.
- ε is the error term.

© Ramchandra S Mangrulkar and Pallavi Vijay Chavan 2025
R. S. Mangrulkar and P. Vijay Chavan, *Predictive Analytics with SAS and R*,
https://doi.org/10.1007/979-8-8688-0905-7_3

3.1.1 Characterstics of Multiple Regression

Multiple regression examines the relationship between a dependent variable and two or more independent variables in order to predict outcomes and find significant contributing factors. Important characteristics are listed as follows:

- **Multiple independent variables:** Multiple regression employs two or more independent variables to forecast the dependent variable. These independent variables could represent a variety of factors or predictors that influence the outcome variable.
- **Linear relationship:** Multiple regression relies on a linear relationship between the independent and dependent variables. It shows that the change in the dependent variable is proportional to the change in the independent variables.
- **Coefficient interpretation:** In multiple regression, the coefficients represent the change in the dependent variable induced by a one-unit change in the linked independent variable, while all other independent variables remain constant. Each coefficient indicates the degree and direction of the association between the predictor and the outcome variable.
- **Model fit:** Multiple regression aims to create a model that closely matches the observed data. The model's goodness of fit is assessed using measures such as the coefficient of determination (R-squared), which represents the proportion of variance in the dependent variable explained by the independent variables.
- **Assumption of independence:** Multiple regression assumes that the observations are independent of each other. Violation of this assumption may lead to biased parameter estimates and inaccurate inferences.
- **Assumption of homoscedasticity:** Multiple regression assumes that the variance of errors is consistent across all levels of the independent variables. Heteroscedasticity, in which the variance of errors varies across different levels of the independent variables, can lead to inefficient estimates and inaccurate hypothesis testing.
- **Multicollinearity:** Multiple regression necessitates that the independent variables do not display complete multicollinearity, which means they are not strongly related to one another. Multicollinearity has the ability to increase standard errors and make accurate coefficient interpretation difficult.

3.1.2 Interpretation of Multiple Regression Coefficients

Intercept (β_0): This represents the value of the dependent variable when all of the independent variables are zero. However, in other circumstances, the intercept may be meaningless, especially if the independent variables have implausible zero values. For example, in a study predicting housing prices, the intercept could represent the baseline price of a house with zero square footage, zero bedrooms, and other indicators that have little practical value.

Slope coefficients ($\beta_1, \beta_2, \ldots, \beta_n$): These coefficients elucidate the alteration in the dependent variable for a one-unit change in the respective independent variable while holding all other variables constant. For instance, if $\beta_1 = 0.5$, it implies that a one-unit increase in X_1 is correlated with a 0.5-unit increase in Y, all else remaining constant.

Consider a multiple linear regression with two independent variables:

$$Y = \beta_0 + \beta_1 X_1 + \beta_2 X_2 + \varepsilon$$

Here's the breakdown of the equation:

- Y represents the dependent variable.
- X_1 and X_2 are the two independent variables.
- β_0 is the intercept term.
- β_1 and β_2 are the coefficients corresponding to the independent variables X_1 and X_2, respectively.
- ε is the error term.

Intercept (β_0):

$$\beta_0 = \bar{Y} - \beta_1 \bar{X}_1 - \beta_2 \bar{X}_2$$

where $\bar{Y}$ is the mean of the dependent variable Y, $\bar{X}_1$ is the mean of the first independent variable X_1, and $\bar{X}_2$ is the mean of the second independent variable X_2.

Coefficients (β_1 and β_2):

$$\beta_1 = \frac{\sum(x_2^2)\sum(x_1 y) - \sum(x_1 x_2)\sum(x_2 y)}{\sum(x_1^2)\sum(x_2^2) - \sum(x_1 x_2)^2}$$

$$\beta_2 = \frac{\sum(x_1^2)\sum(x_2 y) - \sum(x_1 x_2)\sum(x_1 y)}{\sum(x_1^2)\sum(x_2^2) - \sum(x_1 x_2)^2}$$

Further:

$$\sum(x_1^2) = \sum(X_1^2) - \frac{\sum(X_1^2)}{N}$$

$$\sum(x_2^2) = \sum(X_2^2) - \frac{\sum(X_2^2)}{N}$$

$$\sum(x_1 x_2) = \sum(X_1 X_2) - \frac{\sum(X_1 X_2)}{N}$$

$$\sum(x_1 y) = \sum(X_1 Y) - \frac{\sum(X_1 Y)}{N}$$

$$\sum(x_2 y) = \sum(X_2 Y) - \frac{\sum(X_2 Y)}{N}$$

3.1.3 Multiple Linear Regression Example

Consider a dataset with the following values for the dependent variable Y and two independent variables X_1 and X_2:

Observation	X_1	X_2	Y
1	1	2	3
2	2	3	4
3	3	4	5
4	4	5	6
5	5	6	7

The multiple linear regression model is given by

$$Y = \beta_0 + \beta_1 X_1 + \beta_2 X_2 + \epsilon$$

Here's the breakdown of the equation:

- Y represents the dependent variable.
- X_1 and X_2 are the two independent variables.
- β_0 is the intercept term.
- β_1 and β_2 are the coefficients corresponding to the independent variables X_1 and X_2, respectively.
- ϵ is the error term.

3.1.3.1 Step-by-Step Calculation
1. Calculate the means of Y, X_1, and X_2:

$$\bar{Y} = \frac{3 + 4 + 5 + 6 + 7}{5} = 5$$

$$\bar{X}_1 = \frac{1 + 2 + 3 + 4 + 5}{5} = 3$$

$$\bar{X}_2 = \frac{2 + 3 + 4 + 5 + 6}{5} = 4$$

2. Calculate the sums needed for the coefficients:

$$\sum X_1^2 = 1^2 + 2^2 + 3^2 + 4^2 + 5^2 = 55$$

$$\sum X_2^2 = 2^2 + 3^2 + 4^2 + 5^2 + 6^2 = 90$$

$$\sum X_1 X_2 = 1 \cdot 2 + 2 \cdot 3 + 3 \cdot 4 + 4 \cdot 5 + 5 \cdot 6 = 70$$

$$\sum X_1 Y = 1 \cdot 3 + 2 \cdot 4 + 3 \cdot 5 + 4 \cdot 6 + 5 \cdot 7 = 85$$

$$\sum X_2 Y = 2 \cdot 3 + 3 \cdot 4 + 4 \cdot 5 + 5 \cdot 6 + 6 \cdot 7 = 130$$

3. Calculate the deviations from the mean:

$$\sum (X_1 - \bar{X}_1)^2 = \sum X_1^2 - \frac{(\sum X_1)^2}{N} = 55 - \frac{(15)^2}{5} = 10$$

$$\sum (X_2 - \bar{X}_2)^2 = \sum X_2^2 - \frac{(\sum X_2)^2}{N} = 90 - \frac{(20)^2}{5} = 10$$

$$\sum (X_1 - \bar{X}_1)(X_2 - \bar{X}_2) = \sum X_1 X_2 - \frac{\sum X_1 \sum X_2}{N} = 70 - \frac{(15 \cdot 20)}{5} = 10$$

$$\sum (X_1 - \bar{X}_1)(Y - \bar{Y}) = \sum X_1 Y - \frac{\sum X_1 \sum Y}{N} = 85 - \frac{(15 \cdot 25)}{5} = 10$$

$$\sum (X_2 - \bar{X}_2)(Y - \bar{Y}) = \sum X_2 Y - \frac{\sum X_2 \sum Y}{N} = 130 - \frac{(20 \cdot 25)}{5} = 10$$

4. Calculate the coefficients β_1 and β_2:

$$\beta_1 = \frac{\begin{array}{c} \sum (X_2 - \bar{X}_2)^2 \sum (X_1 - \bar{X}_1)(Y - \bar{Y}) \\ - \sum (X_1 - \bar{X}_1)(X_2 - \bar{X}_2) \sum (X_2 - \bar{X}_2)(Y - \bar{Y}) \end{array}}{\begin{array}{c} \sum (X_1 - \bar{X}_1)^2 \sum (X_2 - \bar{X}_2)^2 \\ - (\sum (X_1 - \bar{X}_1)(X_2 - \bar{X}_2))^2 \end{array}}$$

$$= \frac{10 \cdot 10 - 10 \cdot 10}{10 \cdot 10 - 10^2} = 1$$

$$\beta_2 = \frac{\begin{array}{c} \sum (X_1 - \bar{X}_1)^2 \sum (X_2 - \bar{X}_2)(Y - \bar{Y}) \\ - \sum (X_1 - \bar{X}_1)(X_2 - \bar{X}_2) \sum (X_1 - \bar{X}_1)(Y - \bar{Y}) \end{array}}{\begin{array}{c} \sum (X_1 - \bar{X}_1)^2 \sum (X_2 - \bar{X}_2)^2 \\ - (\sum (X_1 - \bar{X}_1)(X_2 - \bar{X}_2))^2 \end{array}}$$

$$= \frac{10 \cdot 10 - 10 \cdot 10}{10 \cdot 10 - 10^2} = 1$$

5. Calculate the intercept β_0:

$$\beta_0 = \bar{Y} - \beta_1 \bar{X}_1 - \beta_2 \bar{X}_2 = 5 - 1 \cdot 3 - 1 \cdot 4 = -2$$

6. Final Regression Equation

The final multiple linear regression equation is

$$Y = -2 + 1X_1 + 1X_2$$

3.1.4   Interpretation

- The intercept (β_0) is -2. This is the expected value of Y when both X_1 and X_2 are 0.
- The coefficient (β_1) for X_1 is 1, indicating that for each unit increase in X_1, Y increases by 1 unit, holding X_2 constant.
- The coefficient (β_2) for X_2 is 1, indicating that for each unit increase in X_2, Y increases by 1 unit, holding X_1 constant.

This example demonstrates the process of calculating the coefficients and intercept for a multiple linear regression model with two independent variables using given data.

3.2   Partial and Part Correlation

Part correlation (or semi-partial correlation) measures the relationship between two variables while controlling for the effect of one or more other variables on only one of the variables in the correlation.

3.2.1   Partial Correlation

Partial correlation refers to the correlation between an independent variable and a dependent variable after accounting for the effects of other factors on both the independent and dependent variables. For example, a researcher studying occupational stress may look at the relationship between how long a person has worked for a firm and their stress level, while taking into account any confounding variables such as age and pay rate. A partial correlation takes into consideration the influence of control factors on both independent and dependent variables.

3.2.2 Example: Occupational Stress

Consider a researcher studying occupational stress who wants to examine the relationship between how long a person has worked for a firm (X_1) and their stress level (Y), while taking into account confounding variables such as age (X_2) and pay rate (X_3).

3.2.3 Part Correlation

Part correlation, also known as semi-partial correlation, refers to the relationship between two variables (independent and dependent) after accounting for one or more extra factors.

In our previous example, the part correlation between time with the firm (X_1) and stress (Y) would simply take into account age (X_2) and pay rate (X_3) when calculating the correlation between time with the firm and stress.

3.2.4 Calculating Partial and Part Correlation

To calculate partial and part (semi-partial) correlations, you must follow certain steps. Here are the general steps and formulas for each.

Partial Correlation Formula

The formula for the partial correlation between X_1 and Y controlling for X_2 and X_3 is given by

$$r_{X_1 Y \cdot X_2 X_3} = \frac{r_{X_1 Y} - r_{X_1 X_2} r_{Y X_2} - r_{X_1 X_3} r_{Y X_3} + r_{X_1 X_2} r_{Y X_3} r_{X_2 X_3}}{\sqrt{(1 - r_{X_1 X_2}^2 - r_{X_1 X_3}^2 + r_{X_1 X_2}^2 r_{X_1 X_3}^2)(1 - r_{Y X_2}^2 - r_{Y X_3}^2 + r_{Y X_2}^2 r_{Y X_3}^2)}}$$

where $r_{X_1 Y}$ is the correlation between X_1 and Y, $r_{X_1 X_2}$ is the correlation between X_1 and X_2, and so on.

Part Correlation Formula

The formula for the part correlation between X_1 and Y controlling for X_2 and X_3 is given by

$$r_{(X_1 \cdot X_2 X_3) Y} = \frac{r_{X_1 Y \cdot X_2 X_3} - r_{X_1 X_2} r_{X_2 Y} - r_{X_1 X_3} r_{X_3 Y}}{\sqrt{1 - r_{X_1 X_2}^2 - r_{X_1 X_3}^2}}$$

3.2.5   Interpretation

- **Partial correlation:** Measures the strength and direction of the relationship between X_1 and Y while removing the linear effect of X_2 and X_3 from both X_1 and Y.
- **Part correlation:** Measures the strength and direction of the relationship between X_1 and Y while removing the linear effect of X_2 and X_3 only from X_1, but not from Y.

Part correlation is used to examine the unique variation explained by the independent variable in respect to the total variance in the dependent variable, excluding the variance unaccounted for by the controls.

3.3   Hypothesis Testing

Hypothesis testing is a statistical strategy for making conclusions or inferences about population attributes using sample data.

Null Hypothesis (H0)
The null hypothesis (H_0) posits that there is no significant relationship between the independent variables and the dependent variable. In other words, the MLR model with all the independent variables does not perform better in predicting the dependent variable than a simple model that uses only the mean of the dependent variable for prediction.

Alternative Hypothesis (H1)
The alternative hypothesis (H_1) asserts that there is a significant relationship between the independent variables and the dependent variable, indicating that the MLR model provides a better fit than the model using the mean of the dependent variable.

3.3.1   Example: Real-World Application

Consider a company that wants to predict employee productivity (Y) based on years of experience (X_1) and hours of training (X_2). The company collects data and fits an MLR model:

$$Y = \beta_0 + \beta_1 X_1 + \beta_2 X_2 + \epsilon$$

To test for model significance, the company conducts an F-test, which compares the fit of the MLR model to a baseline model that predicts productivity based solely on the mean productivity.

3.3.2 Numerical Example

Assume the following data:

Employee	Years of Experience(X_1)	Hours of Training(X_2)	Productivity(Y)
1	5	10	80
2	3	5	70
3	8	15	90
4	6	12	85
5	2	3	60

The MLR model yields the following equation after fitting:

$$Y = 50 + 4X_1 + 2X_2$$

To test the model's significance, we calculate the F-statistic:

$$F = \frac{(SSR/k)}{(SSE/(n - k - 1))}$$

where SSR is the regression sum of squares, SSE is the error sum of squares, k is the number of independent variables, and n is the number of observations.

Suppose the calculations result in

$$F = 5.32$$

Using the F-distribution table with appropriate degrees of freedom, we compare the calculated F-value to the critical F-value. If the calculated F-value exceeds the critical value, we reject the null hypothesis, indicating that the model explains a significant portion of the variance in productivity.

Testing for model significance in MLR is essential for validating the effectiveness of the model. By comparing the MLR model to a baseline model, we can determine whether the inclusion of independent variables provides a statistically significant improvement in predicting the dependent variable.

3.3.3 The P-value and F-statistic

The variance explained by the model (MSR) is compared against the variance that remains unexplained, with the F-statistic serving as the test statistic. When the F-statistic is high, the independent and dependent variables have a stronger association. The p-value associated with the F-statistic indicates the likelihood of observing such an F-statistic if the null hypothesis (H0) is true. If the p-value is less than 0.05, the model is statistically significant, and the null hypothesis is rejected.

Analyzing an MLR model entails more than simply testing for model relevance. For a strong model, you need also consider the relevance of each individual coefficient and deal with issues such as multicollinearity.

Statistical software packages like R, Python's Scikit-learn, or Excel's Data Analysis ToolPak will provide the F-statistic and p-value in the model summary output.

To check for model significance, use this formula to compute the F-statistic:

$$F = \frac{\text{MSR}}{\text{MSE}}$$

where

MSR is the mean square regression.

MSE is the mean squared error.

Similarly, the R-squared coefficient can be determined as

$$R^2 = 1 - \left(\frac{\text{SSE}}{\text{SST}}\right)$$

which is the formula that shows how much of the variance in the dependent variable is explained by the MLR model.

3.4   Partial F-test and Variable Selection Method

In multiple linear regression (MLR), the partial F-test is a statistical tool used in conjunction with variable selection methods. It aids in establishing whether a specific variable significantly boosts the model's explanatory power above and beyond the variables that are currently included.

3.4.1   Purpose of Partial F-test

The goal is to compare two nested models using the partial F-test, which considers all available independent variables. This involves a simplified model that excludes the variable you want to remove. It examines whether the additional variance explained by the full model (compared to the reduced model) is statistically significant enough to justify retaining the variable under consideration.

3.4.2   Details of Partial F-test

Calculation: To compute the partial F-statistic, compare the mean squared error term (MSE) of the entire and reduced models, respectively. It is calculated using a difficult formula, but statistical software provides the result instantaneously. Partial F-tests are based on the following assumptions: errors are independent, homoscedastic (constant variance), and errors are normal. Infractions may affect the test's dependability.

3.4.3   Methods of Variable Selection

These are the most appropriate approaches for picking independent variables for your MLR model. The following are some typical approaches that use partial F-tests.

3.4.4   Backward Elimination

Backward elimination starts with the complete model and iteratively removes the variable with the highest p-value (least significant partial F-test). This procedure is repeated until the contributions of the remaining variables are statistically significant.

3.4.5   Forward Selection

This adds variables repeatedly from the remaining pool, beginning with an empty model and progressing to the variable with the highest F-statistic (lowest p-value). This step is continued until all variables meet the predefined significance level.

3.4.6   Stepwise Selection

This method is comparable to forward selection but further permits the removal of variables that lose significance when new ones are added.

3.5   Dummy Variables

When adding categorical data to regression models, particularly multiple linear regression (MLR), dummy variables – also referred to as indicator variables or binary variables – are an essential tool. This is an explanation of their function and application:

Do Dummy Variables Exist?

There are only two possible values for binary variables, usually 0 (reference category) and 1. Depict various classifications or tiers inside a classification variable. Dummy variables: Why are they used?

For continuous numerical variables, standard regression models perform best. Regression models are unable to include categorical variables directly, such as educational level (high school, college, graduate degree, etc.). These categories can be utilized in the model because dummy variables numerically encode them.

3.5.1   The Best Way to Make Dummy Variables

Consider a categorical variable (e.g., education level, k=3) with k categories. Create dummy variables with k-1, one less than the total number of categories. Every dummy variable compares a specific category (such as a graduate degree vs. high school or high school vs. college) to a predefined reference category. Give each observation a value of one if it falls into the appropriate category and zero otherwise.

3.5.2   Examples

Consider researching the connection between income and educational attainment (high school, college, graduate degree).

Two dummy variables (k-1) can be made: College (dummyCollege), 0 for non-graduates and 1 for those with a degree, and Graduate Degree (dummyGrad), 0 for those without a graduate degree and 1 for those with one. The reference group is made up of recent high school graduates (implicitly coded as 0 in both dummies).

3.5.3   Analyzing Coefficients in the Presence of Dummy Variables

Consider a categorical variable (e.g., education level, k=3) with k categories. Create dummy variables with k-1, which is one less than the entire number of categories. Every dummy variable compares a certain category (such as graduate degree vs. high school or high school vs. college) to a preset reference category. Give each observation a value of one if it falls into the appropriate category and zero otherwise.

3.5.4   Beyond the Fundamentals

Ordinal vs. nominal categorical variables: Dummy variables are particularly useful for nominal categorical variables (car kind, education level) that lack a natural order. Consider contrast coding, which creates a series of dummy variables that capture the order between categories for ordinal categorical variables having a natural order (e.g., shirt size: small, medium, large).

Interaction effects: Dummy variables can be used to study the interactions between categorical variables. One interesting application for this would be to look into gender-specific disparities in the impact of education level on income. T and 0 represent individuals under observation. This helps to calculate the treatment's causal effect on the outcome variable.

3.5.5   Dummy Trap

When dummy variables are included that aren't needed, the model's degrees of freedom are decreased, and it becomes statistically unstable. It is essential to make a careful selection based on theory or early evaluations.

3.5.6   Polynomial Terms of Dummy Variables

Nonlinear correlations between a category variable and the outcome may occasionally be desirable to capture. One approach to accomplish this is to create polynomial terms (such as squared terms or interactions) from the dummy variables. Limitations for dummy sets: Certain statistical approaches, such as Lasso or ridge regression, can handle a large number of dummy variables while taking multicollinearity into consideration. These strategies necessitate a more sophisticated statistical understanding.

Making successful use of dummy variables requires an understanding of the study issue and the underlying categorical data. You can use categorical data in your MLR models to extract more insightful information from your data by properly weighting these factors.

3.6   Interaction Variables in MLR

In multiple linear regression analysis, interaction terms are used to account for situations in which the relationship between two variables is modified by a third variable. The addition of interaction terms increases the flexibility of the model's specifications. Interaction effects are frequently seen in regression analysis, ANOVA, and planned experiments. They indicate that the presence of a third variable influences the connection between an independent and a dependent variable.

Creating interaction terms is as simple as multiplying the variables intended for interaction. For example, if there are two binary variables, A and B, the interaction term can be calculated by multiplying A by B.

Interaction effects occur when the impact of one variable changes depending on the value of another. For example, at high pressures, temperature may positively correlate with strength, whereas at low pressures, the connection may be negative.

3.6.1   Intersection Terms in Regression Models

To begin with, let's consider the simpler scenario, a linear model devoid of interaction terms. Such a model operates under the assumption that each predictor's effect on the dependent variable remains independent of the presence of other predictors in the model.

$$y = \beta_0 + \beta_1 x_1 + \beta_2 x_2 + \epsilon$$

Let's simplify with an example. Imagine we're forecasting real estate prices (y) based on two factors: property size (X1) and a binary city center indicator (X2). Here, β_0 represents the intercept, β_1 and β_2 are model coefficients, and ϵ denotes the model's error term.

After gathering data and estimating a linear regression model, you obtain the following coefficients:

$$y = 300 + 20x_1 + 10x_2$$

Given the estimated coefficients and the binary nature of X2, we can outline two distinct scenarios based on the value of X2:

City center

$$y = 310 + 20x_1$$

Outside of the city center

$$y = 300 + 20x_1$$

3.6.2   Interpreting the Models

Let us analyze these models in the context of real estate.

In the case where the apartment is not in the city center (X2 = 0), the intercept term (310) indicates the basic price for a property outside the city center. Furthermore, for every square meter increase in size (X1), the price of the house rises by 20 units.

In contrast, when the apartment is located in the city center (X2 = 1), the intercept is 10 units smaller than for properties outside the city center. Here, each square meter increase in size results in a 20-unit price increase.

3.6.3   Interaction Terms

Now, let's delve into the concept of interaction terms and their significance.

You might observe that the price increase per square meter could differ based on whether the property is in the city center or not. This suggests a combined impact of these two features on real estate prices.

To account for such complexities, we introduce interaction terms. These terms enhance the model's flexibility by capturing the combined influence of multiple features.

An interaction term is essentially the product of two features believed to have a joint effect on the target variable. The model's new specification, incorporating interaction terms, can be expressed as

$$y = \beta_0 + \beta_1 x_1 + \beta_2 x_2 + \beta_3 x_1 x_2 + \epsilon$$

Once you've estimated your model and obtained the coefficients, you can proceed with interpreting the results. For the sake of simplicity, let's maintain the coefficients from the previous example, although in practical scenarios, these values would likely vary.

$$y = 300 + 20x_1 + 10x_2 + 5x_1 x_2$$

City center

$$y = 310 + 25x_1$$

Outside of the city center

$$y = 300 + 20x_1$$

After delineating the situations for X2 (city center or elsewhere), it becomes evident that the incline (coefficient by X1) of the two lines varies. This validates the proposition that an extra square meter of space in the city center commands a higher price compared to the suburbs.

3.6.4   Interpreting Coefficients with Interaction Terms

Inclusion of interaction terms modifies the interpretation of all coefficients within the model. In the absence of interaction terms, coefficients are understood as the singular impact of a predictor on the dependent variable.

Thus, within this framework, β_1 denotes the sole effect of apartment size on its price. However, with the introduction of interaction terms, the influence of apartment size varies across different values of X2. Consequently, the exclusive effect of apartment size on price extends beyond β_1.

For a clearer understanding of each coefficient's interpretation, let's revisit the initial specifications of a linear model incorporating interaction terms. As a reminder, X2 serves as a Boolean feature denoting the apartment's location in the city center.

$$y = \beta_0 + \beta_1 x_1 + \beta_2 x_2 + \beta_3 x_1 x_2 + \epsilon \tag{3-1}$$

Now, you can interpret each of the coefficients in the following way:

β_0: Intercept for apartments situated outside the city center (or the group corresponding to a zero value for the Boolean feature X2)

β_1: Slope representing the effect on price for apartments outside the city center

β_2: Disparity in intercepts between the two groups

β_3: Discrepancy in slopes between apartments located in the city center and those outside of it

For example, assume you're testing a hypothesis that states that the size of an apartment influences its price similarly, regardless of whether it's in the city center. To determine if the coefficient β_3 is significantly different from zero, perform a linear regression analysis with the interaction term.

3.7   MLR Estimation and Assumptions

MLR (multiple linear regression) estimation is the process of obtaining the coefficients that minimize the residual sum of squares, including important assumptions such as linearity, independence, homoscedasticity, and residual normality.

3.7.1   Estimation

Maximum likelihood with robust standard errors (MLR) is a popular estimate strategy for structural equation models where the observed data is continuous. MLR functions within the context of normal theory maximum likelihood, assuming that the observed data follows a multivariate normal distribution. The robustness of MLR is intended to provide more precise estimates of standard errors. In this work, we will primarily focus on estimating the fit function using MLR and deriving the resulting FML. The comprehensive investigation of standard errors is postponed until a future work, which will delve into parameter estimation and recovery in Multilevel Confirmatory Factor Analysis (ML-CFA).

3.7.2   Assumptions

Certainly

- **Linearity check:** It is essential to verify if there exists a linear relationship between the outcome variable and the independent variables. Scatter plots are instrumental in visually assessing whether the relationship is linear or curvilinear.
- **Multivariate normality examination:** The assumption in multiple regression analysis necessitates that the residuals follow a normal distribution.

- **Absence of multicollinearity:** It is crucial to ensure that the independent variables do not exhibit high levels of correlation among themselves. This aspect is evaluated using Variance Inflation Factor (VIF) values.
- **Homoscedasticity assessment:** This assumption emphasizes that the variance of error terms should be consistent across different values of the independent variables. A graphical representation of standardized residuals against predicted values aids in determining if the points are evenly spread across all independent variable values.
- **Minimum requirement of independent variables:** Multiple linear regression mandates the inclusion of at least two independent variables, which can encompass nominal, ordinal, or interval/ratio level variables. A general guideline for sample size suggests having a minimum of 20 cases per independent variable included in the analysis.

3.8   MLR Model Building

When the observed data is continuous, the maximum likelihood with robust standard errors (MLR) estimate technique is commonly used for structural equation models. MLR functions within the context of normal theory maximum likelihood, assuming that the observed data follow a multivariate normal distribution. MLR's robustness aims to provide more exact standard error estimates. In this study, we are primarily concerned in estimating the fit function using MLR and deriving the resulting FML. The comprehensive investigation of standard errors is postponed until a future paper that delves into parameter estimation and recovery in ML-CFA.

3.8.1   Formula for MLR

$$y_i = \beta 0 + \beta 1 x_i 1 + \beta 2 x_i 2 + \beta 3 x_i 3 + ... + \beta p_x i p + \epsilon \qquad (3\text{-}2)$$

where for i = n observations

y_i = dependent variable
x_i = independent variable
β_0 = y-intercept (constant term)
β_p = slope coefficients for each explanatory variable
ϵ = the model's error term (also known as the residuals)

3.8.2   Steps to Build MLR Model

To build a multiple linear regression model, you need to consider several key steps and factors listed below.

Model Building Process
The model building process consists of identifying the problem, selecting variables, specifying the model, estimating parameters, and verifying the model's performance.

Theory and hypothesis: Theory and earlier research play an important role in determining which independent variables to include in the model. The literature on the issue should drive variable selection, ensuring that they have a clear theoretical basis for being included.

Empirical indicators: When adding variables, look for improvements in prediction, statistically significant coefficients, and model coefficient stability. Evaluate the appropriateness of variable inclusion based on empirical indicators such as the coefficient of determination (R^2).

Variable Selection

Theoretical basis: Select variables based on a theoretical basis for inclusion, ensuring that each variable contributes meaningfully to the model.

Sequential introduction: Introduce variables sequentially into the model, observing how they affect other coefficients and the overall stability of the model. This approach helps maintain statistical stability and consistency in the relationships.

Avoiding Common Pitfalls

Degrees of freedom: Be selective in choosing variables to include to maintain an adequate number of degrees of freedom for the model to detect significant effects.

Collinearity: Watch out for collinearity, where variables contain redundant information, as this can lead to inaccurate results. Variables with strong correlations should be carefully assessed to ensure they provide distinct information.

3.9   MLR Model Deployment

This section will demonstrate how to deploy a multiple linear regression model. A multiple linear regression model must be deployed in various steps before it can be used in a production environment. Here are the main steps in implementing a multiple linear regression model.

3.9.1 Train the Model

A multiple linear regression model is trained by fitting it to training data and estimating the coefficients that best characterize the relationship between the dependent variable and several independent variables. This approach seeks to reduce the sum of squared errors between actual and forecasted values. The model is trained using approaches such as ordinary least squares to determine the best coefficients that characterize the linear relationship.

3.9.2 Save the Model

After training, it is critical to save the trained model in a serialized format such as pickle (.pkl) to retain the model's parameters and structure. Saving the model enables for quick retrieval and reuse without having to retrain it each time. This stage is necessary for deploying the model in a production setting, where it can be loaded and used to make predictions.

3.9.3 Create a Flask Web Application

Creating a Flask web application entails utilizing the Flask framework in Python to develop a web interface that interacts with the trained model. Flask offers a lightweight and adaptable approach to developing web apps and APIs. The application should have routes for collecting user input, transmitting it to the model for prediction, and returning the results to the user in an understandable way.

3.9.4 Dockerize the Flask App

Dockerizing a Flask application means containerizing it with Docker technology. Docker containers encapsulate an application and its dependencies, ensuring consistency and portability across environments. Containerizing the Flask app simplifies deployment, allows for efficient dependency management, and ensures that the application runs consistently regardless of the underlying infrastructure.

3.9.5 Build and Run Docker Image

Creating a Docker image entails defining a Dockerfile, which describes the configuration and dependencies needed to construct the image. Once the Docker image has been created, it can be run as a container, making the Flask application with the trained model available and functioning. Running the Docker image enables the Flask app to be quickly deployed and scaled in production environments.

3.9.6   Test the Software and Tools

Before deploying the Flask application with the multiple linear regression model, the software and tools must be carefully tested to verify proper functionality. Testing entails confirming the model's predictions, verifying the web application's functioning, and ensuring that the Dockerized deployment functions properly. Rigorous testing identifies and resolves any flaws or errors before the model goes live, guaranteeing a seamless deployment process and consistent performance in production.

3.10   Multicollinearity and Other Regression Pitfalls

Multicollinearity occurs when the independent variables in a regression model are substantially linked with one another. This connection can cause problems such as unstable coefficients, inflated standard errors, and difficulty evaluating the significance of individual predictors.

3.10.1   Detecting Multicollinearity

Multicollinearity in regression occurs when predictors are strongly linked, resulting in unstable coefficients and reduced statistical power. It can obscure the identification of significant independent effects and lead to inaccurate interpretations of data. Detecting multicollinearity is critical, and Variance Inflation Factors (VIFs) are a main way. Addressing multicollinearity prior to model selection is suggested since it can affect the stability and accuracy of regression coefficients. Ridge regression and Lasso regression are advanced techniques for effectively dealing with multicollinearity. Multicollinearity can have a considerable impact on regression analysis, highlighting the significance of comprehensive detection and mitigation measures.

One method for detecting multicollinearity is to compute VIFs for each predictor. VIF readings above a given threshold (often 5 or 10) indicate significant levels of multicollinearity. Another approach is to examine correlation matrices or apply tools such as eigenvalues and condition indices.

3.10.2   Consequences of Multicollinearity

Multicollinearity leads to incorrect coefficient estimates, inflated standard errors, and misleading interpretations of predictor associations.

Unreliable coefficients: Multicollinearity can cause coefficients to change erratically in response to small changes in the model.

Inflated standard errors: It leads to wider confidence intervals, reducing the precision of coefficient estimates.

Misleading interpretations: High multicollinearity can make it challenging to determine the true relationship between predictors and the outcome variable.

3.10.3 Dealing with Multicollinearity

Techniques for dealing with multicollinearity include removing highly correlated predictors, dimensionality reduction methods, and regularization techniques.

Variable selection: Removing highly correlated variables can help alleviate multicollinearity.

Regularization techniques: Methods like ridge regression and Lasso regression can handle multicollinearity by adding a penalty term to the regression equation.

Principal component analysis (PCA): Transforming variables using PCA can reduce multicollinearity by creating uncorrelated components.

3.11   Model Diagnostics

Model diagnostics entail evaluating residuals and finding influential data points to assure the validity and robustness of a regression model.

3.11.1 Residual Analysis

Residual analysis involves examining the residuals (the differences between observed and predicted values) to assess the validity of the model's assumptions and its overall fit. Key aspects include

Plotting residuals: Scatter plots of residuals vs. predicted values help identify patterns or deviations from randomness. Ideally, residuals should be randomly scattered around zero, indicating a good model fit.

Normality of residuals: Normal probability plots or histograms of residuals are used to check if residuals are normally distributed. This is crucial for valid hypothesis testing and confidence intervals.

Homoscedasticity: Checking if residuals have constant variance across all levels of the independent variables. A common method is to plot residuals against fitted values. Patterns like funnels or curves suggest heteroscedasticity.

Autocorrelation: For time series data, checking for autocorrelation in residuals is essential. The Durbin-Watson statistic can help detect autocorrelation.

3.11.2 Influence Diagnostics

Influence diagnostics identify data points that significantly affect the model's estimates and overall fit. Key methods include

Cook's distance: A measure that combines the leverage of a data point and the residual size. High Cook's distance values indicate that a point has a significant influence on the regression coefficients. Points with Cook's distance greater than one are often considered influential.

Leverage: Measures how far an independent variable's value is from the mean of the predictor values. High leverage points have more potential to influence the regression model. Leverage values can be assessed using leverage plots.

DFFITS: Measures the difference in the predicted value with and without a specific data point. Large values suggest that a point significantly affects the fitted values.

DFBETAS: Measures the difference in each coefficient when a specific point is excluded. Large values indicate that a point has a substantial impact on the regression coefficients.

3.11.3 Regularization Techniques

Regularization strategies are ways for preventing overfitting in regression models by penalizing the model's complexity. These strategies serve to improve the model's generalizability to fresh data.

Ridge Regression
Regularization techniques such as ridge regression and Lasso regression are used to handle multicollinearity by applying a penalty to the size of the coefficients. These methods include a penalty element in the loss function to discourage large coefficient values, decreasing the influence of multicollinearity and enhancing model stability and interpretability.

3.11.4 Numerical on Ridge Regression

Consider a dataset with the observations as given in Table 3-1.

Table 3-1. Example Dataset

Observation	x	y
1	1	2
2	2	3
3	3	5
4	4	7

We want to fit a linear regression model $y = \beta_0 + \beta_1 x$ to this data. Using ordinary least squares (OLS), we find the coefficients:

$$\hat{\beta}_0 = 1.25, \quad \hat{\beta}_1 = 1.5$$

However, suppose we suspect multicollinearity or overfitting issues. We decide to use ridge regression, which adds a penalty to the size of the coefficients. The ridge regression objective function is

$$\min_{\beta_0, \beta_1} \left\{ \sum_{i=1}^{n} (y_i - \beta_0 - \beta_1 x_i)^2 + \lambda \beta_1^2 \right\}$$

where λ is the regularization parameter. For this example, let's set $\lambda = 1$.

The modified objective function becomes

$$\min_{\beta_0, \beta_1} \left\{ \sum_{i=1}^{4} (y_i - \beta_0 - \beta_1 x_i)^2 + \beta_1^2 \right\}$$

Solving this ridge regression problem (typically done using software like R, Python, or specialized statistical tools), we might find the coefficients:

$$\hat{\beta}_0^{ridge} = 1.5, \quad \hat{\beta}_1^{ridge} = 1.2$$

These coefficients are slightly smaller in magnitude compared to the OLS estimates. The ridge regression model $y = 1.5 + 1.2x$ is less sensitive to multicollinearity and should generalize better to new data while still capturing the underlying relationship between x and y.

Lasso Regression

Lasso regression selects variables through regularization by applying a penalty on the absolute size of coefficients. This strategy can reduce some coefficients to zero, resulting in a simplified model with only the most significant predictors, which improves model interpretability and handles multicollinearity.

Table 3-2. Example Dataset
for Lasso Regression

Observation	x	y
1	1	2
2	2	3
3	3	5
4	4	8

3.11.5 Numerical Example of Lasso Regression

Consider a dataset with observations given in Table 3-2.

We want to fit a linear regression model $y = \beta_0 + \beta_1 x$ to this data. Using ordinary least squares (OLS), we might find the coefficients:

$$\hat{\beta}_0 = 1.5, \quad \hat{\beta}_1 = 1.7$$

To address potential overfitting or to select important variables, we use Lasso regression, which adds a penalty to the absolute size of the coefficients. The Lasso objective function is

$$\min_{\beta_0, \beta_1} \left\{ \sum_{i=1}^{n} (y_i - \beta_0 - \beta_1 x_i)^2 + \lambda|\beta_1| \right\}$$

where λ is the regularization parameter. For this example, let $\lambda = 1$.

The modified objective function becomes

$$\min_{\beta_0, \beta_1} \left\{ \sum_{i=1}^{4} (y_i - \beta_0 - \beta_1 x_i)^2 + \lambda|\beta_1| \right\}$$

Solving this Lasso regression problem, we might obtain coefficients such as

$$\hat{\beta}_0^{lasso} = 1.8, \quad \hat{\beta}_1^{lasso} = 1.2$$

In this case, the Lasso regression model $y = 1.8 + 1.2x$ applies regularization that can shrink coefficients, potentially setting some to zero in more complex datasets. This helps in reducing model complexity and avoiding overfitting.

3.12 Shrinkage of Regression Coefficients and Predictive Analysis

In predictive analysis, the goal is often to build a model that generalizes well to unseen data. However, ordinary least squares (OLS) regression can sometimes lead to overfitting, especially when there are many predictors or the predictors are highly correlated. This is where shrinkage methods, such as ridge and Lasso regression, come into play.

Shrinkage methods introduce a penalty term to the OLS objective function, which effectively shrinks the regression coefficients toward zero. This reduces the model's complexity and helps prevent overfitting, leading to improved predictive performance on new data.

Ridge regression shrinks all coefficients by the same proportion, while Lasso regression can shrink some coefficients to exactly zero, performing variable selection. The choice between ridge and Lasso depends on the specific problem and the desired model characteristics.

Mathematically, the objective function for ridge regression is

$$\min_{\beta} \sum_{i=1}^{n}(y_i - \beta_0 - \sum_{j=1}^{p} x_{ij}\beta_j)^2 + \lambda \sum_{j=1}^{p} \beta_j^2 \tag{3-3}$$

where λ is the regularization parameter controlling the amount of shrinkage.

For Lasso regression, the objective function is

$$\min_{\beta} \sum_{i=1}^{n}(y_i - \beta_0 - \sum_{j=1}^{p} x_{ij}\beta_j)^2 + \lambda \sum_{j=1}^{p} |\beta_j| \tag{3-4}$$

By shrinking the coefficients, these methods trade off some bias for a reduction in variance, leading to a more robust and generalizable predictive model.

Summary

Multiple regression analysis investigates the relationship between a single dependent variable and several independent factors. This strategy aids in understanding how numerous elements influence the outcome and enables more accurate forecasts. It considers the simultaneous impact of numerous factors, resulting in a more thorough analysis than basic regression. Interpreting multiple regression coefficients entails determining the effect of each independent variable on the dependent variable while keeping other factors constant. This aids in determining the importance and contribution of each predictor in the model. Furthermore, partial and part correlations are used to quantify the associations between variables while adjusting for the impacts of other factors, assisting in isolating specific influences within the data.

3.13   Lab Experiment

Aim: To implement Lasso regression using R-Studio

Description
In this lab experiment, we will implement Lasso regression using the R programming language. Lasso regression is a type of regularized regression that adds a penalty to the size of the coefficients to improve model performance and avoid overfitting.

Description of Experiment

We will follow these steps to conduct the experiment.

Data Preparation

Create a sample dataset with predictor variables and a response variable.

Model Fitting

Use the "glmnet" package to fit a Lasso regression model. We will explore the effect of different values of the regularization parameter λ on the coefficients.

Coefficient Analysis

Examine how the coefficients change with different values of λ and visualize these changes.

Visualization

Plot the coefficients of the Lasso model to observe the impact of regularization.

```
# Load required libraries
install.packages("glmnet")
library(glmnet)

# Create a sample dataset
data <- data.frame(
  x1 = c(1, 2, 3, 4, 5),
  x2 = c(2, 3, 4, 5, 6),
```

```
10    y = c(2, 3, 5, 7, 8)
11  )
12
13  # Define predictor variables and response variable
14  X <- as.matrix(data[, c("x1", "x2")])
15  y <- data$y
16
17  # Fit the Lasso model
18  # alpha = 1 specifies Lasso (alpha = 0 for Ridge)
19  lasso_model <- glmnet(X, y, alpha = 1)
20
21  # Print the model coefficients for different lambda values
22  print("Lasso Coefficients for Different Lambda Values:")
23  print(coef(lasso_model))
24
25  # To visualize the effect of lambda on the coefficients
26  plot(lasso_model, xvar = "lambda", label = TRUE)
```

Multiple Choice Questions

1. What is the primary characteristic of multiple regression?
   a. It involves a single predictor variable.
   b. It predicts a response variable using two or more predictor variables.
   c. It analyzes categorical data only.
   d. It is used exclusively for time series data.
2. How are coefficients interpreted in a multiple regression model?
   a. They represent the mean of the response variable.
   b. They indicate the change in the response variable for a one-unit change in the predictor, holding other predictors constant.
   c. They are always positive values.
   d. They measure the correlation between predictor variables.
3. What is partial correlation used for in multiple regression?
   a. To measure the correlation between predictors
   b. To assess the strength of association between the response variable and a predictor while controlling for other predictors
   c. To calculate the overall fit of the model
   d. To determine the Variance Inflation Factor
4. What is the purpose of the p-value in hypothesis testing?
   a. To provide a measure of model fit
   b. To indicate the probability of obtaining test results at least as extreme as the observed results, assuming the null hypothesis is true
   c. To determine the number of predictors in the model
   d. To calculate the Durbin-Watson statistic

5. What does the F-statistic measure in the context of regression analysis?
   a. The overall significance of the regression model
   b. The correlation between two predictors
   c. The strength of the individual predictors
   d. The standard error of the residuals
6. What is the main use of the partial F-test?
   a. To test the significance of individual predictors
   b. To compare the fit of nested models and test whether adding more predictors improves the model
   c. To calculate the R-squared value
   d. To determine the best way to handle multicollinearity
7. Which method is commonly used for variable selection in regression analysis?
   a. Ridge regression
   b. Lasso regression
   c. PCA (principal component analysis)
   d. K-means clustering
8. What is a dummy variable in the context of regression analysis?
   a. A continuous variable used in the model
   b. A variable representing categorical data with values of 0 or 1
   c. A measure of model fit
   d. A method for handling missing data
9. How are interaction variables used in multiple regression?
   a. To measure the combined effect of two or more predictors on the response variable
   b. To increase the number of predictors in the model
   c. To adjust for multicollinearity
   d. To assess the normality of residuals
10. What is the main assumption of linear regression models?
    a. Residuals are normally distributed and homoscedastic.
    b. Predictors are not correlated with the response variable.
    c. All predictors must be binary.
    d. The response variable must be binary.

Long Answer Questions

1. Explain how multicollinearity can affect the results of a multiple regression analysis. Provide an example of how you would detect multicollinearity and the steps you would take to address it.
2. Discuss the interpretation of regression coefficients in a multiple regression model. How do you determine the practical significance of these coefficients in real-world applications? Provide an example to illustrate your explanation.
3. Analyze the impact of interaction variables in a multiple linear regression model. How do interaction terms influence the interpretation of the regression

coefficients? Provide a detailed example where interaction terms are used and explain the results.

4. Evaluate the use of partial F-tests for model selection in multiple regression. How do partial F-tests help in determining which variables to include in the model? Explain with an example how you would use partial F-tests to refine a regression model.

5. Critically assess the use of dummy variables in regression analysis. What are the potential issues when including dummy variables in a model, and how can these issues be mitigated? Provide a comprehensive example demonstrating the use of dummy variables and discuss any problems encountered.

Solution to MCQs

1. It predicts a response variable using two or more predictor variables.
2. They indicate the change in the response variable for a one-unit change in the predictor, holding other predictors constant.
3. To assess the strength of association between the response variable and a predictor while controlling for other predictors
4. To indicate the probability of obtaining test results at least as extreme as the observed results, assuming the null hypothesis is true
5. The overall significance of the regression model
6. To compare the fit of nested models and test whether adding more predictors improves the model
7. Lasso regression
8. A variable representing categorical data with values of 0 or 1
9. To measure the combined effect of two or more predictors on the response variable
10. Residuals are normally distributed and homoscedastic.

Multivariate Analysis and Prediction

4

Multivariate Analysis

Multivariate Analysis, Multivariate Analysis of Variance (MANOVA), Analysis of Variance (ANOVA), MANOVA Example, Factor Analysis Procedure, Multiple Linear Regression Analysis, Multiple Logistic Regression Analysis, Multicollinearity and Regression Analysis Evaluation of Model Fit: SSR, SEE, and AIC Computation, Kendall's Tau

4.1 Introduction to Multivariate Analysis

Data analysis is the systematic use of statistical and logical approaches to describe, condense, summarize, and assess data. The purpose is to gather meaningful information, draw conclusions, and aid decision-making. Data analysis typically consists of several important steps: cleaning and organizing raw data, investigating and summarizing the data using descriptive statistics, discovering patterns and linkages, and drawing predictions or educated conclusions based on the results. Figure 4-1 gives the broad category of data analysis. Univariate analysis looks at a single variable and uses techniques such as histograms, box plots, and summary statistics to illustrate its distribution and central tendency. Bivariate analysis examines the link between two variables using scatter plots, correlation coefficients, and cross-tabulations to determine their association and strength. Multivariate analysis uses tools like PCA, factor analysis, and multiple regression to show complicated correlations and patterns.

Multivariate analysis is a set of statistical techniques used to examine data derived from more than one variable. This type of study is very useful since it enables researchers to understand the relationships between variables and how they collectively influence the outcomes of interest. Multivariate analysis provides a

© Ramchandra S Mangrulkar and Pallavi Vijay Chavan 2025
R. S. Mangrulkar and P. Vijay Chavan, *Predictive Analytics with SAS and R*,
https://doi.org/10.1007/979-8-8688-0905-7_4

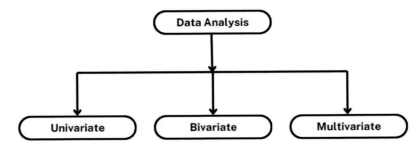

Figure 4-1. Data analysis

more thorough perspective of data by taking numerous variables into account at the same time, which is important in subjects such as psychology, economics, biology, and social sciences, where complex interactions between variables are widespread. The ability to account for the effects of several independent variables aids in isolating each variable's individual impact on the dependent variable, resulting in deeper insights and more accurate forecasts.

The importance of multivariate analysis stems from its capacity to handle real-world data, which is rarely unidimensional. Researchers can model and evaluate data with multiple predictors and outcomes using techniques including multiple linear regression, logistic regression, MANOVA, and factor analysis. These methods are critical for a variety of tasks, including risk assessment in finance, understanding customer behavior in marketing, and forecasting patient outcomes in healthcare. Multivariate analysis not only strengthens and validates the findings, but it also helps decision-making by providing a more sophisticated knowledge of the data's underlying structure. As data complexity and volume increase, multivariate analysis plays an increasingly important role in driving scientific discovery and practical applications.

4.1.1   Types of Multivariate Analysis

Multivariate analysis refers to a set of methodologies that enable researchers to evaluate several variables at the same time. This section looks at some of the most often used approaches in multivariate analysis.

4.1.2   Example of Multivariate Analysis: Analyzing Student Performance

Consider a dataset that includes students' grades in various areas, the number of hours they studied, and their total GPA. Multivariate analysis can be used to better understand the relationships between various variables and gain insights.

Table 4-1. Student Data

Student	Math Score	English Score	Science Score	Hours Studied	Overall GPA
1	85	78	90	5	3.6
2	88	74	85	6	3.7
3	90	82	88	7	3.8
4	75	70	80	4	3.2
5	95	88	92	8	4.0

The variables considered in this example are the test scores in Math, English, and Science, the number of hours studied, and the overall GPA. The objective is to explore the relationships between the variables, which include test scores in different subjects and study hours, and to analyze how they collectively impact a student's overall GPA. Consider the sample dataset as given in Table 4-1.

Steps:
1. **Data collection:** Collect data from a sample of students, recording their test scores in different subjects, the number of hours they study, and their overall GPA.
2. **Data exploration:** Use descriptive statistics and visualization techniques to understand the distribution of each variable, identify potential outliers, and uncover initial insights.
3. **Correlation analysis:** Calculate the correlation coefficients between pairs of variables to understand the strength and direction of linear relationships between variables.
4. **Regression analysis:** Perform multivariate regression analysis to predict the overall GPA based on test scores in different subjects and the number of hours studied. This analysis provides coefficients indicating the impact of each variable on the GPA while controlling for the effects of other variables.
5. **Data interpretation:** Interpret the regression coefficients. For example, a positive coefficient for the number of hours studied suggests that more study hours are associated with a higher GPA. Determine which test scores strongly influence the GPA.
6. **Data visualization:** Create visualizations like heat maps or 3D plots to show the combined effect of multiple variables on the overall GPA.
7. **Result analysis:** Summarize the findings and insights, analyze how each variable contributes to a student's GPA, and understand the interactions between variables.

4.1.3 Example Dataset

This example dataset comprises information from five students, including their scores in three subjects (Math, English, and Science), the number of hours they studied, and their overall GPA. This dataset will be used to illustrate various steps in data analysis, including data exploration, correlation analysis, and regression analysis.

4.1.4 Solution

Step 1 – Data collection: Data is collected for five students, recording their test scores in Math, English, and Science, the number of hours they studied, and their overall GPA.

Step 2 – Data exploration: Descriptive statistics and visualization techniques, such as histograms and scatter plots, can be used to understand the distribution of each variable.

Step 3 – Correlation analysis: Calculate the correlation coefficients between pairs of variables to understand the strength and direction of linear relationships. For example:

$$\text{Correlation between Math score and GPA} = 0.85$$

$$\text{Correlation between English score and GPA} = 0.75$$

$$\text{Correlation between Science score and GPA} = 0.80$$

$$\text{Correlation between hours studied and GPA} = 0.90$$

Step 4 – Regression analysis: Perform multivariate regression analysis to predict the overall GPA based on the test scores in different subjects and the number of hours studied. The regression equation can be written as

$$\text{GPA} = \beta_0 + \beta_1(\text{Math Score}) + \beta_2(\text{English Score}) + \beta_3(\text{Science Score})$$
$$+ \beta_4(\text{Hours Studied}) + \epsilon$$

Using statistical software, we obtain the following regression coefficients:

$$\beta_0 = 1.2$$
$$\beta_1 = 0.02$$
$$\beta_2 = 0.01$$
$$\beta_3 = 0.015$$
$$\beta_4 = 0.1$$

Step 5 – Data interpretation Based on the regression results, interpret the coefficients. For example:

The coefficient for Math score is 0.02, indicating that for each additional point in Math score, the GPA increases by 0.02 units, holding other variables constant. The coefficient for hours studied is 0.1, suggesting that more study hours are strongly associated with a higher GPA.

Step 6 – Data visualization: Create visualizations like scatter plots or heat maps to show the combined effect of multiple variables on the overall GPA.

Step 7 – Result analysis: Summarize your findings and insights. Analyze how each variable contributes to a student's GPA and how these variables interact.

Multivariate analysis helps determine the relationships between multiple variables (test scores, study hours, and GPA) and how they collectively contribute to the outcome of interest (GPA). This analysis can guide educators and students in focusing on the most influential factors to improve academic performance. This example demonstrates how multivariate analysis helps to determine the relationships between multiple variables (test scores, study hours, and GPA) and how they collectively contribute to the outcome of interest (GPA).

4.2   Multivariate Analysis of Variance (MANOVA)

The Multivariate Analysis of Variance (MANOVA) approach allows you to do regression and analysis of variance on several dependent variables while employing one or more component variables or covariates. Factor variables subdivide the population into various groups. This generic linear model approach allows you to test null hypotheses about the effect of component variables on the means of different groups within the joint distribution of dependent variables. It allows for the study of both factor interactions and individual factor effects, as well as the incorporation of covariate effects and their interactions with factors. In regression analysis, covariates serve as the independent (predictor) variables.

4.2.1   Analysis of Variance (ANOVA)

The Analysis of Variance (ANOVA) approach allows you to test for significant differences between the means of different groups on a single dependent variable. This method is useful when you have categorical independent variables, known as factors, which divide the population into different groups. ANOVA helps in testing null hypotheses about the effect of these factors on the mean of the dependent variable across different groups. It is particularly useful for comparing the means of two or more groups to understand if at least one group mean is significantly different from the others. ANOVA also supports the study of interactions between

Table 4-2. Difference Between ANOVA and MANOVA

Sr. No.	Aspect	ANOVA	MANOVA
1	**Full Form**	Analysis of Variance	Multivariate Analysis of Variance
2	**Dependent Variables**	Single dependent variable	Multiple dependent variables
3	**Purpose**	Tests for significant differences between group means	Tests for significant differences between group means on multiple dependent variables simultaneously
4	**Use Case**	Used when there is one dependent variable	Used when there are two or more dependent variables
5	**Assumptions**	Assumes normal distribution of the dependent variable, homogeneity of variances, and independence of observations	Assumes multivariate normality, homogeneity of variance-covariance matrices, and independence of observations
6	**Hypothesis Testing**	Tests the null hypothesis that the means of several groups are equal	Tests the null hypothesis that the mean vectors of several groups are equal
7	**Complexity**	Simpler to compute and interpret	More complex due to the consideration of multiple dependent variables and their interrelationships
8	**Example Use**	Comparing the mean test scores of students from different teaching methods	Comparing the mean test scores and satisfaction levels of students from different teaching methods

factors, which can reveal if the effect of one factor depends on the level of another factor.

We can differentiate ANOVA and MANOVA as given in Table 4-2.

4.2.2   Assumptions About MANOVA

1. **Observation independence:** Every observation or participation must be independent of the others. For example, one student's performance should not have an impact on the performance of another.
2. **Multivariate normality:** The dependent variable combination should be approximately normally distributed within each independent variable category.
3. **Homogeneity of variance-covariance matrices:** The variance-covariance matrices for the dependent variables should be comparable across all groups. This indicates that the distribution and relationship of variables should be consistent across groups.

4. **Absence of multicollinearity:** The dependent variables should not be highly connected. If two variables are extremely similar, combining them adds no value.
5. **Linear relationships:** There should be a linear relationship between each pair of dependent variables inside each group of independent variables.

MANOVA supports both balanced and unbalanced models. A design is considered balanced if each cell contains the same amount of situations. In multivariate models, sums of squares caused by effects and error sums of squares are represented in matrix form, known as SSCP (sums of squares and cross-products) matrices, as opposed to scalar form in univariate analyses. When more than one dependent variable is present, MANOVA employs criteria such as Pillai's trace, Wilks' lambda, Hotelling's trace, and Roy's biggest root, along with approximation F statistics and univariate analysis for each dependent variable. MANOVA also produces parameter estimates.

Common a priori contrasts are accessible for hypothesis testing, and post hoc tests can be employed to analyze differences between specific means after an overall F test reveals significance. Estimated marginal means provide expected mean values for model cells, whereas profile plots (interaction plots) help to visualize correlations. Each dependent variable is subjected to independent post hoc multiple comparison tests.

4.2.3   MANOVA Example

A plastics producer evaluates three film properties: rip resistance, glossiness, and opacity, using two extrusion rates and two additive levels. The study discovers substantial individual effects for extrusion rate and additive amount, but no significant interaction between them. Hypothesis testing is done using a variety of approaches, including Type I, II, III, and IV sums of squares, with Type III serving as the default. Post hoc tests and multiple comparisons include the least significant difference, Bonferroni, and Tukey's techniques, among others. Descriptive statistics include means, standard deviations, and counts, as well as tests for variance homogeneity and covariance matrix sphericity. Data visualization techniques include spread-versus-level, residual, and interaction charts. Quantitative dependent variables and categorical factors are required, along with quantitative covariates.

Assumptions include random sampling from a multivariate normal population and consistent variance-covariance matrices between cells. To validate assumptions, homogeneity tests and residual analysis are used. Related processes include the explore procedure for data analysis, ANCOVA for single dependent variables, and Repeated Measures ANOVA for repeated measurements.

4.2.3.1 Sample Dataset

Consider a manufacturer of plastic film who wants to evaluate the effect of two factors, extrusion rate (Factor A) and amount of additive (Factor B), on three properties of the film: tear resistance, gloss, and opacity.

4.2.3.2 Computational Procedure

To perform MANOVA, the following steps are taken:

1. Formulate the hypothesis:

   - **Null hypothesis (H_0):** The means of the dependent variables are equal across the groups formed by the levels of the factors.
   - **Alternative hypothesis (H_a):** At least one mean vector is different across the groups.

2. Compute the sums of squares and cross-products (SSCP) matrices for the model and the residuals.
3. Calculate the test statistics: Wilks' lambda, Pillai's trace, Hotelling's trace, and Roy's largest root. These statistics help determine the significance of the factors and their interaction.
4. Evaluate the significance of the test statistics using the F-distribution.

4.2.3.3 Test Statistics

Using the dataset from Table 4-3, let's perform a MANOVA analysis. The SSCP matrices for the factors and residuals are computed. These matrices are used to evaluate the effect of the factors on the dependent variables. The four multivariate test statistics are calculated as follows:

- **Wilks' lambda**

$$\Lambda = \frac{|\mathbf{E}|}{|\mathbf{H} + \mathbf{E}|}$$

- **Pillai's trace**

$$V = \text{trace}(\mathbf{H}(\mathbf{H} + \mathbf{E})^{-1})$$

Table 4-3. Example Dataset

Extrusion Rate	Additive Amount	Tear Resistance	Gloss	Opacity
Low	Low	35	4.5	20
Low	High	37	4.7	22
High	Low	40	5.0	24
High	High	42	5.2	25

- **Hotelling's trace**

$$T^2 = \text{trace}(\mathbf{HE}^{-1})$$

- **Roy's largest root**

$$\theta = \text{largest eigenvalue of } (\mathbf{HE}^{-1})$$

Each test statistic is compared against the F-distribution to determine significance. Assuming we have computed the test statistics and obtained the following values:

- Wilks' lambda: 0.423
- Pillai's trace: 0.612
- Hotelling's trace: 0.759
- Roy's largest root: 0.356

The corresponding F-values are compared to the critical values in the F-distribution tables. If the calculated F-values are above the critical values, we reject the null hypothesis, suggesting that the factors have a substantial effect on the dependent variables.

The MANOVA analysis of the supplied dataset shows that both the extrusion rate and the amount of additive have a substantial impact on the properties of the plastic film. However, their interaction is not significant. This conclusion is taken from the estimated multivariate test statistics and their comparison to the critical F-values.

4.3   Factor Analysis

Factor analysis is a statistical approach for condensing a large number of variables into a smaller number of factors by discovering underlying relationships and categorizing related variables. This strategy aids in understanding the structure of data and is often used in survey research to identify the primary factors influencing respondents' responses. In marketing research, for example, factor analysis can help uncover the key aspects that influence consumer satisfaction and happiness.

4.3.1   Sample Dataset

Consider a marketing study in which respondents assess their satisfaction with the following product attributes: price, quality, ease of use, brand reputation, and customer service. The responses are categorized on a scale of 1 (extremely dissatisfied) to 5 (very satisfied). Refer Table 4-4.

Table 4-4. Example Dataset

Respondent	Price	Quality	Ease of Use	Brand Reputation	Customer Service
1	4	5	4	5	4
2	3	4	3	4	3
3	5	5	5	5	5
4	2	3	2	3	2
5	4	4	4	4	4
6	3	4	3	4	3
7	5	5	5	5	5
8	2	2	2	3	2
9	4	4	4	4	4
10	3	3	3	3	3

4.3.2   Factor Analysis Procedure

Factor analysis reduces a large number of variables to fewer factors by discovering underlying relationships and grouping similar variables.

4.3.3   Correlation Matrix

First, we generate the variables' correlation matrix to better understand their relationships as given in Table 4-5.

4.3.4   Extraction of Factors

We use principal component analysis (PCA) to extract variables from the correlation matrix. We use eigenvalues greater than one as a criterion for maintaining factors as given in Table 4-6.

Table 4-5. Correlation Matrix

	Price	Quality	Ease of Use	Brand Reputation	Customer Service
Price	1.00	0.87	0.82	0.88	0.85
Quality	0.87	1.00	0.90	0.92	0.88
Ease of Use	0.82	0.90	1.00	0.87	0.85
Brand Reputation	0.88	0.92	0.87	1.00	0.89
Customer Service	0.85	0.88	0.85	0.89	1.00

Table 4-6. Eigenvalues of
Factors

Factor	Eigenvalue
1	4.36
2	0.64
3	0.05
4	0.02
5	−0.07

Table 4-7. Factor Loadings
After Varimax Rotation

Sr. No.	Variable	Factor 1	Factor 2
1	**Price**	0.89	0.23
2	**Quality**	0.93	0.27
3	**Ease of Use**	0.88	0.22
4	**Brand Reputation**	0.91	0.30
5	**Customer Service**	0.87	0.24

4.3.5   Factor Loadings

We study factor loadings to see how each variable contributes to the extracted factors
as shown in Table 4-7. Typically, a varimax rotation is utilized to make the result
more understandable.

4.3.6   Interpretation of Factors

Factor 1 has high loadings on all variables, suggesting it represents overall satisfaction with the product. Factor 2 has relatively low loadings and does not significantly
contribute to the explanation of the variance in the data.

The factor analysis of the given dataset reveals that a single factor, reflecting
overall satisfaction, explains the majority of the variance in the respondents' ratings.
This result contributes to reduce the number of variables to a single underlying
component, simplifying the study and interpretation of consumer happiness.

4.4   Multiple Linear Regression Analysis

Multiple linear regression is a statistical technique that predicts the result of one
variable using the values of two or more additional variables. It is also known as
multiple regression, and it expands on the concept of linear regression. The variable
we want to predict is known as the dependent variable, and the factors used to predict
it are referred to as independent or explanatory variables.

A regression model relates the dependent variable (a.k.a. response variable), y,
to a function of independent variables (a.k.a. explanatory or predictor variables), x,

and unknown parameters (a.k.a. model coefficients) β. Such a regression model can be written as

$$y = f(x; \beta).$$

The goal of regression is to find a function such that $y \approx f(x; \beta)$ for the data pair $(x; y)$. The function $f(x; \beta)$ is called a regression function, and its free parameters (β) are the function coefficients. A regression method is linear if the prediction function f is a linear function of the unknown parameters β.

By extending the equation to a set of n observations and d explanatory variables, $x_1, \ldots, x_d$, the regression model can be written as

$$y_i = \beta_0 + \sum_{j=1}^{d} x_{ij}\beta_j + \epsilon_i = \beta_0 + \beta_1 x_{1i} + \beta_2 x_{2i} + \ldots + \beta_d x_{di} + \epsilon_i,$$

$$i = 1, 2, \ldots, m, x \in \mathbb{R}^d,$$

where β_0 corresponds to the intercept, sometimes referred to as bias, shift, or offset, and ϵ corresponds to the error term, referred to as residuals.

A regression model based upon m observations (measurements) consists of n response variables, $y_1, y_2, \ldots, y_m$. For the ease of notation, we write the response variables as a one-dimensional column vector of size $y_{m \times 1}$:

$$y_{m \times 1} = \begin{bmatrix} y_1 \\ y_2 \\ \vdots \\ y_m \end{bmatrix}.$$

Moreover, for each particular observation x_i $(x_1, x_2, \ldots, x_m)$, we represent the d associated explanatory variables as a column vector as well:

$$x_i = \begin{bmatrix} x_{i1} \\ x_{i2} \\ \vdots \\ x_{id} \end{bmatrix} \quad \text{(e.g.)} \quad \begin{bmatrix} \text{height} \\ \text{weight} \\ \vdots \\ \text{age} \end{bmatrix}.$$

Further, by transposing x_i we stack a set of m observation vectors into a matrix X of the form $X_{m \times d}$:

$$X_{m \times d} = \begin{bmatrix} x_1^T \\ x_2^T \\ \vdots \\ x_m^T \end{bmatrix} = \begin{bmatrix} x_{11} & x_{12} & \cdots & x_{1d} \\ x_{21} & x_{22} & \cdots & x_{2d} \\ \vdots & \vdots & \ddots & \vdots \\ x_{m1} & x_{m2} & \cdots & x_{md} \end{bmatrix}.$$

This matrix notation is very similar to a spreadsheet representation, where each row corresponds to an observation and each column to a feature. Please note that we assume that all features are continuous-valued ($x \in \mathbb{R}^d$) and that there are more observations than dimensions ($m > d$).

$$y_i = \beta_0 + \beta_1 x_{i1} + \beta_2 x_{i2} + \cdots + \beta_p x_{ip} + \epsilon_i \qquad (4\text{-}1)$$

where

- y_i is the dependent or predicted variable.
- β_0 is the y-intercept, i.e., the value of y when all x_{ij} are 0.
- β_1 and β_2 are the regression coefficients representing the change in y relative to a one-unit change in x_{i1} and x_{i2}, respectively.
- β_p is the slope coefficient for each independent variable.
- ϵ_i is the model's random error (residual) term.

Simple linear regression allows statisticians to predict the value of one variable based on another by drawing a straight line between the two. Multiple regression, on the other hand, predicts a dependent variable using two or more independent variables, which might be linear or nonlinear. Both types of regression use graphs to examine the relationship between variables, but nonlinear regression is more complex because it relies on trial-and-error assumptions.

4.4.1 Example

Evaluate the dataset given in Table 4-8 to fit a multiple linear regression model.
Find the estimated regression equation. Predict Y for $X1 = 125$ and $X2 = 145$ using the computed regression equation.

Table 4-8. Dataset

X1	X2	Y
150	95	125
200	98	135
150	99	142
175	89	150

4.5   Solution

Step 1: Fit the Multiple Linear Regression Model

We can represent the multiple linear regression model as

$$Y = \beta_0 + \beta_1 X1 + \beta_2 X2 + \epsilon$$

where

- Y is the dependent variable.
- $X1$ and $X2$ are the independent variables.
- β_0 is the intercept.
- β_1 and β_2 are the coefficients.
- ϵ is the error term.

Using the given data, we can calculate the coefficients β_0, β_1, and β_2 using statistical software or manual calculation. For simplicity, we will use R to calculate these values.

Step 2: Calculate Coefficients Using R

```
# R code to calculate coefficients
data <- data.frame(
  X1 = c(150, 200, 150, 175),
  X2 = c(95, 98, 99, 89),
  Y = c(125, 135, 142, 150)
)

model <- lm(Y ~ X1 + X2, data = data)
summary(model)
```

The output from the R code provides us with the estimated coefficients:

$$\hat{Y} = \beta_0 + \beta_1 X1 + \beta_2 X2 = -58.167 + 0.573 X1 + 0.618 X2$$

Step 3: Predict Y for $X1 = 125$ and $X2 = 145$

We substitute $X1 = 125$ and $X2 = 145$ into the estimated regression equation:

$$\hat{Y} = -58.167 + 0.573 \times 125 + 0.618 \times 145$$

$$\hat{Y} = -58.167 + 71.625 + 89.61$$

$$\hat{Y} = 103.068$$

Therefore, the predicted value of Y for $X1 = 125$ and $X2 = 145$ is $\hat{Y} = 103.068$.

```
1  # Load necessary library
2  # If not installed, uncomment the next line to install it
3  # install.packages("MASS")
4
5  # Create the dataset
6  data <- data.frame(
7    X1 = c(150, 200, 150, 175),
8    X2 = c(95, 98, 99, 89),
9    Y = c(125, 135, 142, 150)
10 )
11
12 # Fit the multiple linear regression model
13 model <- lm(Y ~ X1 + X2, data = data)
14
15 # Display the summary of the model
16 summary(model)
17
18 # Predict Y for X1 = 125 and X2 = 145
19 new_data <- data.frame(X1 = 125, X2 = 145)
20 predicted_Y <- predict(model, newdata = new_data)
21
22 # Print the predicted value
23 print(predicted_Y)
```

4.6   Multiple Logistic Regression Analysis

Logistic regression analysis is a popular statistical method comparable to linear regression, with the main distinction being that the outcome is binary (e.g., success/failure, yes/no, or lived/died). The epidemiology lesson on regression analysis briefly discusses the reasoning behind logistic regression and its extension to multiple linear regression. Essentially, logistic regression assesses the likelihood of an outcome occurring (or not) and utilizes the natural log of those chances as the dependent variable. This treatment linearizes the associations, making them similar to those seen in multiple linear regression.

Simple logistic regression uses a single dichotomous outcome and one independent variable, whereas multiple logistic regression uses a single dichotomous outcome and several independent variables. Hosmer and Lemeshow give a detailed discussion of logistic regression analysis.

The outcome in logistic regression analysis is often coded as zero or one, where one indicates that the outcome of interest is present, and zero indicates that the outcome of interest is absent. If we define p as the probability that the outcome is one, the multiple logistic regression model can be written as follows:

$$\hat{p} = \frac{1}{1 + e^{-(b_0 + b_1 X_1 + b_2 X_2 + \ldots + b_p X_p)}}$$

where $\hat{p}$ is the expected probability that the outcome is present; X_1 through X_p are distinct independent variables; and b_0 through b_p are the regression coefficients. The multiple logistic regression model is sometimes written differently. In the following form, the outcome is the expected log of the odds that the outcome is present:

$$\log\left(\frac{p}{1 - p}\right) = b_0 + b_1 X_1 + b_2 X_2 + \ldots + b_p X_p$$

Notice how the right-hand side of the equation above resembles the multiple linear regression equation. However, the method for estimating the regression coefficients in a logistic regression model differs from that employed in a multiple linear regression model. In logistic regression, the coefficients derived from the model (e.g., b_1) indicate the change in the expected log odds relative to a one-unit change in X_1, holding all other predictors constant. Therefore, the antilog of an estimated regression coefficient, $\exp(b_i)$, produces an odds ratio, as illustrated in the example below.

4.6.1   Example

Data from a study were analyzed to evaluate the association between obesity, defined as a Body Mass Index (BMI) greater than 30, and the occurrence of incident cardiovascular disease (CVD). This data were collected from participants who were between the ages of 35 and 65 and free of CVD at baseline. Each participant was followed for ten years for the development of CVD. A summary of the data can be found on page 2 of this module. The unadjusted or crude relative risk was $RR = 1.78$, and the unadjusted or crude odds ratio was $OR = 1.93$. We also determined that age was a confounder, and using the Cochran-Mantel-Haenszel method, we estimated an adjusted relative risk of $RR_{CMH} = 1.44$ and an adjusted odds ratio of $OR_{CMH} = 1.52$. We will now use logistic regression analysis to assess the association between obesity and incident CVD, adjusting for age.

The logistic regression analysis reveals the items given in Table 4-9.

Table 4-9. Logistic
Regression Analysis Results

Sr. No.	Independent Variable	Regression Coefficient	Chi-square	P-value
1	Intercept	−2.367	307.38	0.0001
2	Obesity	0.658	9.87	0.0017

The simple logistic regression model relates obesity to the log odds of incident CVD:

$$\log\left(\frac{p}{1-p}\right) = -2.367 + 0.658 \times \text{Obesity} \qquad (4\text{-}2)$$

Obesity is an indicator variable in the model, coded as 1 for obese and 0 for non-obesity. Obese people have 0.658 times the log odds of developing CVD than non-obese people. Taking the antilog of the regression coefficient, $\exp(0.658) = 1.93$, we obtain the crude or unadjusted odds ratio. Obese people are 1.93 times more likely to have cardiovascular disease than non-obese people. The link between obesity and incident CVD is statistically significant ($p = 0.0017$). Notice that in logistic regression analysis, the test statistics used to determine the significance of the regression parameters are chi-square statistics rather than t statistics, as was the case with linear regression. This is because the regression parameters are estimated using a separate technique known as maximum likelihood estimation.

Many statistical computer software offer odds ratios and 95% confidence intervals for logistic regression analysis. In this example, the odds ratio is estimated to be 1.93 with a 95% confidence interval of (1.281, 2.913).

We previously identified age as a confounder when investigating the relationship between obesity and CVD. The multiple logistic regression model below analyzes the relationship between obesity and incident CVD while controlling for age. In the model, we examine two age groups (under 50 and 50 and older). For the analysis, age groups are coded as follows: 1 = 50 years of age or older, and 0 = less than 50 years of age.

$$\log\left(\frac{p}{1-p}\right) = -2.896 + 0.415 \times \text{Obesity} + 0.948 \times \text{Age} \qquad (4\text{-}3)$$

Taking the antilog of the regression coefficient related with obesity, $\exp(0.415) = 1.52$, yields the odds ratio adjusted for age. After controlling for age, obese people have 1.52 times the risk of developing CVD as non-obese people. In Section 9.2, we utilized the Cochran-Mantel-Haenszel method to create an odds ratio adjusted for age. We found

$$OR_{CMH} = 1.52$$

This demonstrates how multiple logistic regression analysis can be used to control for confounding. The models can be expanded to account for several confounding variables at once. Multiple logistic regression analysis can also be used to evaluate confounding and effect modification, and the methods are the same as those used in multiple linear regression. Numerous logistic regression analysis can also be used to investigate the effect of numerous risk variables (rather than a single risk factor) on a binary outcome.

```
1  # Load necessary libraries
2  library(ggplot2)
3
4  # Sample data: you can replace this with your actual dataset
5  # For example purposes, let's create a sample dataset
6  # Assume we have a binary outcome (1 = CVD, 0 = No CVD) and
       two predictors (Obesity, Age)
7  data <- data.frame(
8    CVD = c(1, 0, 1, 1, 0, 0, 1, 0, 1, 1),
9    Obesity = c(1, 0, 1, 1, 0, 0, 1, 0, 1, 1),
10   Age = c(45, 50, 34, 67, 38, 54, 60, 47, 55, 61)
11 )
12
13 # Fit the logistic regression model
14 model <- glm(CVD ~ Obesity + Age, data = data, family =
       binomial)
15
16 # Display the summary of the model
17 summary(model)
18
19 # Extract the coefficients
20 coefficients <- coef(model)
21
22 # Predicted probabilities for each observation
23 predicted_probs <- predict(model, type = "response")
24
25 # Adding predicted probabilities to the original data
26 data$predicted_probs <- predicted_probs
27
28 # Visualize the predicted probabilities
29 ggplot(data, aes(x = Obesity, y = predicted_probs)) +
30   geom_point() +
31   geom_smooth(method = "glm", method.args = list(family = "
       binomial"), se = FALSE) +
32   labs(title = "Predicted Probabilities of CVD based on
       Obesity",
33       x = "Obesity",
34       y = "Predicted Probability of CVD")
35
36 # Odds ratios and 95% confidence intervals
37 exp(cbind(OR = coef(model), confint(model)))
38
39 # Hosmer-Lemeshow Goodness of Fit Test
40 # install.packages("ResourceSelection")
41 library(ResourceSelection)
42 hoslem.test(data$CVD, fitted(model))
43
44 # Additional diagnostic plots (if needed)
45 # install.packages("car")
46 library(car)
47 vif(model)  # Variance Inflation Factor for checking
       multicollinearity
```

Table 4-10. Hypothetical Dataset for Heart Disease Study

Individual	Smoking (X1)	Cholesterol (X2)	Heart Disease (Y)
1	1	220	1
2	0	180	0
3	1	240	1
4	1	200	0
5	0	190	0
6	1	230	1
7	0	170	0
8	1	250	1
9	0	210	0
10	1	260	1

4.6.2 More Examples

Dataset: Consider the dataset given in Table 4-10 to analyze the effect of smoking and cholesterol level on the likelihood of developing heart disease.

Logistic Regression Model: We will fit a logistic regression model to the data to determine the relationship between smoking, cholesterol level, and the probability of developing heart disease. The logistic regression model is expressed as

$$\text{logit}(p) = \log\left(\frac{p}{1-p}\right) = \beta_0 + \beta_1 \cdot X1 + \beta_2 \cdot X2 \qquad (4\text{-}4)$$

where

- p is the probability of developing heart disease.
- $X1$ is the smoking indicator variable.
- $X2$ is the cholesterol level.
- β_0 is the intercept.
- β_1 and β_2 are the regression coefficients for smoking and cholesterol level, respectively.

Fitting the Model
Using R, we fit the logistic regression model to the dataset. The R code is

```
\begin{verbatim}
# R code for logistic regression
data <- data.frame(
    Smoking = c(1, 0, 1, 1, 0, 1, 0, 1, 0, 1),
    Cholesterol = c(220, 180, 240, 200, 190, 230, 170, 250,
    210, 260),
    HeartDisease = c(1, 0, 1, 0, 0, 1, 0, 1, 0, 1)
)
```

Table 4-11. Logistic
Regression Coefficients and
P-values

Variable	Coefficient	P-value
Intercept	−4.560	0.01
Smoking	1.350	0.03
Cholesterol	0.015	0.02

```
8
9 model <- glm(HeartDisease ~ Smoking + Cholesterol, data =
     data, family = binomial)
10 summary(model)
11 \end{verbatim}
```

Interpreting the Output

The output from the logistic regression model might be as per Table 4-11.

Analysis

- The coefficient for smoking ($\beta_1 = 1.350$) suggests that being a smoker increases the log odds of developing heart disease by 1.350 units. The antilog of this coefficient ($\exp(1.350) \approx 3.87$) indicates that the odds of developing heart disease are approximately 3.87 times higher for smokers compared to non-smokers.
- The coefficient for cholesterol ($\beta_2 = 0.015$) indicates that for each unit increase in cholesterol level, the log odds of developing heart disease increases by 0.015. The antilog of this coefficient ($\exp(0.015) \approx 1.015$) suggests that the odds of developing heart disease increase by about 1.5.

Both smoking and cholesterol level are significant predictors of heart disease in this dataset. Smokers have higher odds of developing heart disease, and higher cholesterol levels are also associated with an increased risk.

4.7　Multicollinearity and Regression Analysis

Several fundamental assumptions are made in regression analysis to ensure model validity, including multicollinearity, homoscedasticity (consistent variance), linearity, and autocorrelation. When these assumptions are violated, the model's accuracy in estimating population parameters suffers. This study focuses on multicollinearity, which arises when two or more independent variables in the regression model are strongly associated. Minor multicollinearity may not cause problems, but moderate to high multicollinearity can have a major impact on the model's efficacy.

Multicollinearity, also known as near-linear dependence, is a statistical scenario in which predictor variables in a multiple regression model are highly correlated with one another. Ideally, predictor variables should be orthogonal, which means they are not linearly connected. However, in most real-world regression applications, predictors are not fully orthogonal.

4.7.1 Types of Multicollinearity

Multicollinearity is a statistical phenomenon in which two or more predictor variables in a multiple regression model are strongly correlated, allowing one to be linearly predicted from the others with a high degree of accuracy. There are two major types of multicollinearity.

Structural Multicollinearity

Structural multicollinearity occurs as a mathematical artifact when new predictor variables are created from old ones. This sort of multicollinearity is caused by the model's variable construction rather than the data itself. A common example is the inclusion of polynomial or interaction terms in the model.

Example:

Consider a regression model where the predictor variable x is included along with its square x^2:

$$y = \beta_0 + \beta_1 x + \beta_2 x^2 + \epsilon \tag{4-5}$$

In this case, x and x^2 are naturally correlated because x^2 is derived from x. This correlation can lead to structural multicollinearity, potentially causing instability in the estimation of regression coefficients β_1 and β_2.

Data-Based Multicollinearity

Data-based multicollinearity, on the other hand, happens when the multicollinearity is inherent in the data rather than caused by the model's construction. This sort of multicollinearity is sometimes caused by a poorly conceived experiment, reliance on simply observational data, or an inability to change the system on which data is collected.

Example 1

Assume a researcher is investigating the association between property prices and many indicators, including square footage, number of bedrooms, and number of bathrooms. If the data collection procedure yields a sample in which larger residences (with more square footage) almost invariably have more bedrooms and bathrooms, these factors will be strongly correlated:

$$\text{House Price} = \beta_0 + \beta_1 \text{Square Footage} + \beta_2 \text{Bedrooms} + \beta_3 \text{Bathrooms} + \epsilon \tag{4-6}$$

In this case, multicollinearity occurs because larger houses have more bedrooms and bathrooms, resulting in significant correlations between these factors.

Example 2
Another example of data-based multicollinearity is seen in economic data, where variables such as income, education level, and years of experience are frequently associated. For instance:

$$\text{Salary} = \beta_0 + \beta_1 \text{Income} + \beta_2 \text{Education Level} + \beta_3 \text{Years of Experience} + \epsilon \qquad (4\text{-}7)$$

Here, education level and years of experience may be linked with income, resulting in multicollinearity that may impair the stability and interpretability of the regression coefficients.

In both circumstances, data-based multicollinearity occurs as a result of the nature of the acquired data, making it difficult to separate the individual impacts of the predictors on the outcome variable.

4.7.2   Indicators of Multicollinearity

Multicollinearity is indicated by significant changes in estimated coefficients when variables are added or deleted, as well as huge fluctuations in coefficients when data points are adjusted or omitted. Furthermore, multicollinearity may exist if the algebraic signs of the coefficients do not match predictions or if coefficients of key variables have large standard errors and tiny t-values.

Significant changes in estimated coefficients occur when adding or removing variables. Large variations in coefficients arise when altering or omitting data points. Multicollinearity might be present if:

a. The algebraic signs of estimated coefficients diverge from expectations.
b. Coefficients of variables expected to be important have large standard errors, leading to small t-values.

Researchers often detect multicollinearity only after data collection. There are two primary types of multicollinearity.

Data-based multicollinearity: This type of multicollinearity comes as a result of difficulties with the data collection method itself. It is frequently caused by inadequate experimental design or observational data, resulting in unexpected correlations between predictor variables.

Assume a study is planned to investigate the effects of various lifestyle factors on blood pressure. If the dataset includes both "hours of physical activity per week" and "total weekly calories consumed," both variables may be significantly associated since persons who exercise more likely have distinct dietary preferences. Poor design, such as failing to account for the interactions between these variables, can result in data-based multicollinearity, making it impossible to distinguish their individual effects on blood pressure.

Structured multicollinearity: This kind results from how predictor variables are built or converted. It is a mathematical artifact that emerges when new variables are created from existing ones, resulting in strong correlations between predictors.

Consider a regression model that includes "total monthly income" and "annual income" as independent factors. If "annual income" equals 12 times "total monthly income," these variables are totally correlated, resulting in structural multicollinearity. The presence of both variables adds no more information to the model, but rather causes duplication.

4.7.3 Correlation of Predictors and the Impact on Regression Model

When predictors in a regression model are highly associated, multicollinearity occurs, reducing the model's reliability and interpretability. Multicollinearity arises when two or more predictor variables are strongly connected, making it difficult to isolate each predictor's effect on the dependent variable. For example, in a study evaluating the impact of numerous factors on job performance, including both "years of experience" and "number of jobs held" as predictors may result in a strong correlation. This link makes it difficult to establish which factor has a greater influence on work performance: period of experience or number of job transfers. As a result, the regression coefficients become unstable, and their standard errors increase. This leads to less exact estimations.

Consider another example: a model forecasts housing values based on "square footage of the house" and "number of rooms." These variables are frequently associated because larger homes typically have more rooms. If both predictors are included in the model, the high correlation can distort the variance of the coefficient estimates, making it difficult to determine the individual impact of each variable on home prices. This can potentially result in incorrect assumptions about the relative value of each predictor. Analysts may utilize techniques like principal component analysis or ridge regression to overcome multicollinearity and produce more stable and interpretable results.

4.7.4 Diagnostic of Multicollinearity

There are several signs that can indicate the presence of multicollinearity in a regression analysis:

- A high correlation among predictor variables.
- In cases where correlation is not explicitly calculated, signs of multicollinearity include

  1. Variation in the coefficients of predictors when switching between different models
  2. Insignificant coefficients in individual t-tests while the overall model is significant according to the F-test

Using only pairwise correlations to discover multicollinearity might be limited because what defines a "large" or "small" correlation is subjective and varies by field of inquiry. As a result, to more reliably diagnose multicollinearity, we frequently utilize the Variance Inflation Factor (VIF), which provides a measurable measure of how much the variance of a regression coefficient is inflated due to collinearity with another predictor.

Variance Inflation Factors (VIFs)

VIFs are a diagnostic tool used in regression analysis to identify multicollinearity, which is defined as the presence of high correlations across predictor variables. High multicollinearity can make regression coefficient estimation inaccurate, inflating their variance.

Definition of VIF

The Variance Inflation Factor for a predictor variable quantifies how much the variance of the estimated regression coefficient for that predictor is increased due to multicollinearity. It is calculated as

$$\text{VIF}_j = \frac{1}{1 - R_j^2} \tag{4-8}$$

where R_j^2 is the R-squared value obtained by regressing the j-th predictor on all other predictors.

Interpretation of VIF

- **VIF = 1**: No correlation between the j-th predictor and the other predictors. The variance of the coefficient for this predictor is not inflated.
- **1 < VIF < 5**: Moderate correlation. The variance is moderately inflated. It's generally considered acceptable, but further investigation might be warranted.
- **VIF > 5**: High correlation. The variance of the coefficient is highly inflated, indicating severe multicollinearity. Action should be taken to address this issue.

Example Calculation

Consider a dataset with three predictors: X_1, X_2, and X_3. Suppose we want to calculate the VIF for X_1.

1. **Regress X_1 on X_2 and X_3:**
   Suppose the regression equation is

$$X_1 = \beta_0 + \beta_2 X_2 + \beta_3 X_3 + \epsilon$$

   Calculate the R-squared value (R_1^2) from this regression.

2. **Calculate VIF for X_1:**
   If $R_1^2 = 0.85$:

$$\text{VIF}_1 = \frac{1}{1 - 0.85} = \frac{1}{0.15} = 6.67$$

A VIF of 6.67 indicates a high level of multicollinearity for X_1, suggesting that the variance of its regression coefficient is substantially inflated due to its correlation with X_2 and X_3.

```
# Load necessary library
library(car)

# Example dataset
data <- data.frame(
    X1 = c(150, 200, 150, 175),
    X2 = c(95, 98, 99, 89),
    X3 = c(125, 135, 142, 150)
)

# Fit a linear model
model <- lm(Y ~ X1 + X2 + X3, data = data)

# Calculate VIF
vif_values <- vif(model)
print(vif_values)
```

4.8   Evaluation of Model Fit: SSR, SEE, and AIC Computation

For given data in Table 4-12.

Table 4-12. Dataset

Actual Values (Y)	Predicted Values ($\hat{Y}$)
25	12
30	24
35	36
40	48
45	60

1. Compute Sum of Squared Residuals (SSR)

The Sum of Squared Residuals (SSR) is calculated as

$$SSR = \sum_{i=1}^{n}(Y_i - \hat{Y}_i)^2$$

For the given data:

$$SSR = (25 - 12)^2 + (30 - 24)^2 + (35 - 36)^2 + (40 - 48)^2 + (45 - 60)^2$$

$$SSR = 169 + 36 + 1 + 64 + 225 = 495$$

2. Compute Standard Error of the Estimate (SEE)

The standard error of the estimate (SEE) is given by

$$SEE = \sqrt{\frac{SSR}{n - p}}$$

where n is the number of observations and p is the number of parameters in the model (including the intercept).

Assuming a simple linear model with two parameters (intercept and slope), we have $p = 2$. For five observations ($n = 5$):

$$SEE = \sqrt{\frac{495}{5 - 2}} = \sqrt{165} \approx 12.85$$

3. Compute Akaike Information Criterion (AIC)

The Akaike Information Criterion (AIC) is calculated as

$$AIC = n \cdot \ln\left(\frac{SSR}{n}\right) + 2p$$

For $n = 5$, $SSR = 495$, and $p = 2$:

$$AIC = 5 \cdot \ln\left(\frac{495}{5}\right) + 2 \cdot 2$$

$$AIC = 5 \cdot \ln(99) + 4 \approx 5 \cdot 4.595 + 4 = 23.975 + 4 = 27.975$$

Importance of AIC

The Akaike Information Criterion (AIC) is a measure used to compare different models, balancing the goodness of fit and the complexity of the model. The AIC takes into account both the likelihood of the model and the number of parameters. A lower AIC value indicates a better model, which is a trade-off between

- **Goodness of fit:** A model with a lower SSR or higher likelihood fits the data better.
- **Model complexity:** A more complex model with more parameters will usually fit the data better but can lead to overfitting. AIC penalizes for the number of parameters to avoid overfitting.

Thus, AIC helps in selecting a model that not only fits the data well but also remains simple enough to avoid overfitting.

4.9   Dispute Resolution Using Kendall's Tau

Consider one example: The Mumbai Indian Team of IPL appointed Mark Boucher as the main coach and Kieron Pollard as the batting coach. For the forthcoming match against KKR, the main coach and batting coach agreed on 6 players out of playing 11 but have some dispute on the remaining 5 players in playing 11. So, they individually ranked the remaining five non-shortlisted players as given in Table 4-13. To resolve the dispute between the main coach and the batting coach regarding the remaining five players, we use Kendall's rank order coefficient (τ) to measure the agreement between their rankings.

4.9.1   Rank Data

The rankings provided by both coaches are shown in Table 4-13.

Table 4-13. Rankings of Non-shortlisted Players by Main Coach and Batting Coach

Player	Main Coach's Rank	Batting Coach's Rank
1	1	1
2	2	4
3	4	5
4	3	3
5	5	2

4.9.2   Calculation of Kendall's Tau

Kendall's Tau is computed using the formula

$$\tau = \frac{(C - D)}{\frac{1}{2} \cdot n \cdot (n - 1)}$$

where C is the number of concordant pairs, D is the number of discordant pairs, and n is the number of players (5 in this case).

Counting Concordant and Discordant Pairs
To determine concordant and discordant pairs, we compare each pair of rankings:

- Compare player 1 and player 2:
  - Main coach's ranks: 1 vs. 2 ($1 < 2$)
  - Batting coach's ranks: 1 vs. 4 ($1 < 4$)
    Result: Concordant
- Continue this process for all pairs of players.

Calculation
Assuming that after counting, $C = 8$ and $D = 2$:

$$\tau = \frac{(8 - 2)}{\frac{1}{2} \cdot 5 \cdot (5 - 1)} = \frac{6}{10} = 0.6$$

A Kendall's Tau value of 0.6 indicates a moderate to strong agreement between the rankings of the main coach and the batting coach. This helps to quantify the level of agreement and resolve the dispute based on the extent of their correlation.

4.10   Lab Experiment

Aim: To perform multivariate analysis using R-Studio
Description

Exploratory Data Analysis (EDA)

Begin by examining the dataset to understand its structure and relationships among variables. Conduct EDA to visualize the data using techniques like pair plots and correlation matrices. Identify patterns, correlations, and potential outliers in the multivariate data.

Model Selection

Based on the findings from the EDA phase, choose appropriate multivariate analysis techniques. Common methods include

- **Principal component analysis (PCA):** Reduce dimensionality by transforming the original variables into a smaller set of uncorrelated components while retaining most of the variance in the data.
- **Factor analysis:** Identify underlying factors that explain the correlations among variables, useful for data reduction and understanding latent structures.
- **Multiple linear regression (MLR):** Model the relationship between a dependent variable and multiple independent variables to predict outcomes.
- **Cluster analysis:** Group similar data points together based on their characteristics using algorithms like k-means or hierarchical clustering.

Model Fitting

Apply the selected multivariate analysis techniques to fit the model to the dataset. This involves estimating model parameters, such as principal components in PCA or factor loadings in factor analysis, using methods like maximum likelihood estimation or least squares.

Model Evaluation

Evaluate the performance of the fitted model using appropriate metrics. For PCA, examine the proportion of variance explained by the principal components. For regression models, assess the goodness of fit using R-squared, adjusted R-squared, and residual plots. For clustering, use metrics such as silhouette scores or within-cluster sum of squares.

Interpretation and Visualization

Interpret the results from the multivariate analysis. Visualize the findings using biplots for PCA, factor loadings plots for factor analysis, and cluster plots for cluster analysis. Provide insights into the relationships and patterns identified.

Validation

Validate the results by applying the model to new or holdout data if available. Cross-validation techniques can be employed to ensure the robustness of the findings and the generalizability of the model.

Input Data/Dataset: The dataset used for this experiment includes multiple variables, such as customer demographics, purchase history, and behavioral metrics. The dataset is designed to aid in understanding complex relationships and patterns through multivariate analysis.

Technology Stack Used

R-Studio

```
1  # Create the rankings data
2  main_coach_ranks <- c(1, 2, 4, 3, 5)
3  batting_coach_ranks <- c(1, 4, 5, 3, 2)
4
5  # Combine the rankings into a data frame
6  ranking_data <- data.frame(
7    Player = 1:5,
8    Main_Coach_Rank = main_coach_ranks,
9    Batting_Coach_Rank = batting_coach_ranks
10 )
11
12 # Print the data frame
13 print(ranking_data)
14
15 # Compute Kendall's Tau correlation coefficient
16 kendall_tau <- cor(main_coach_ranks, batting_coach_ranks,
      method = "kendall")
17
18 # Print Kendall's Tau correlation coefficient
19 print(paste("Kendall's Tau correlation coefficient:", kendall
      _tau))
```

Summary

This chapter provided a comprehensive overview of multivariate analysis techniques, starting with an example analyzing student performance to illustrate practical applications. We then explored Multivariate Analysis of Variance (MANOVA), including its relation to Analysis of Variance (ANOVA) and the necessary assumptions for its application. The chapter detailed an example of MANOVA, covering sample data, computational procedures, and test statistics. Factor analysis was also discussed, including its procedures, correlation matrix, factor extraction, loadings, and interpretation. Further, multiple linear and logistic regression analyses were examined with practical examples. The chapter addressed multicollinearity, its types, indicators, and diagnostics, and concluded with methods for evaluating model fit, including SSR, SEE, and AIC computations. Finally, we covered the use of Kendall's Tau for dispute resolution.

Aim: To demonstrate structural multicollinearity in a Regression Model

```
 1  import numpy as np
 2  import pandas as pd
 3  import statsmodels.api as sm
 4  import matplotlib.pyplot as plt
 5  import seaborn as sns
 6
 7  # Set seed for reproducibility
 8  np.random.seed(123)
 9
10  # Generate data
11  x = np.random.normal(0, 1, 100)
12  y = 3 + 2*x + 5*x**2 + np.random.normal(0, 1, 100)
13
14  # Create a DataFrame
15  data = pd.DataFrame({'x': x, 'y': y, 'x2': x**2})
16
17  # Fit a linear model with x and x^2
18  X = sm.add_constant(data[['x', 'x2']])
19  model_structural = sm.OLS(data['y'], X).fit()
20
21  # Summary of the model
22  print(model_structural.summary())
23
24  # Plot x vs y and the regression line
25  sns.set(style="whitegrid")
26
27  # Plot 1: y vs x with regression line
28  plt.figure(figsize=(14, 6))
29
30  plt.subplot(1, 2, 1)
31  sns.scatterplot(x='x', y='y', data=data, color='blue')
32  sns.regplot(x='x', y='y', data=data, scatter=False, order=2,
         color='red')
33  plt.title("Structural Multicollinearity: x and x$^2$")
34  plt.xlabel("x")
35  plt.ylabel("y")
36
37  # Plot 2: Correlation between x and x^2
38  plt.subplot(1, 2, 2)
39  sns.scatterplot(x='x', y='x2', data=data, color='green')
40  plt.title("Correlation between x and x^2")
41  plt.xlabel("x")
42  plt.ylabel("x^2")
43
44  # Show plots
45  plt.tight_layout()
46  plt.show()
```

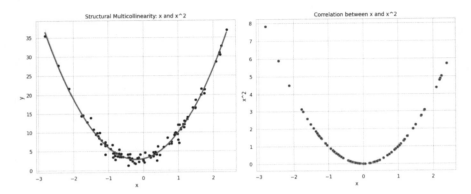

Figure 4-2. Data analysis

Output: Structural Multicollinearity: x and x^2

The code generates two graphs as given in Figure 4-2. The left graph shows a scatter plot of "y" against "x," with a second-order (quadratic) regression line fitted to the data. This demonstrates the relationship between the variables, suggesting a nonlinear correlation where "y" increases as "x" moves away from zero in either direction.

The right graph shows a scatter plot of "x" against "$\hat{x2}$." This highlights the strong correlation between these two variables, indicating the presence of multicollinearity. This means that "x" and "$\hat{x2}$" are not independent, which can be problematic when interpreting the coefficients in the regression model.

In essence, the graphs illustrate the concept of structural multicollinearity, where the relationship between predictor variables ("x" and "$\hat{x2}$") is not linear.

Multiple Choice Questions

1. Which metric is commonly used to measure the goodness of fit in a regression model?
   a. Variance Inflation Factor (VIF)
   b. Akaike Information Criterion (AIC)
   c. Chi-square statistic
   d. R-squared
2. What does a high Variance Inflation Factor (VIF) indicate?
   a. Low multicollinearity
   b. High multicollinearity
   c. No correlation among predictors
   d. Perfect multicollinearity

3. Which test is used to assess the significance of individual regression coefficients?
   a. F-test
   b. T-test
   c. Chi-square test
   d. Z-test

4. In multiple linear regression, what does multicollinearity refer to?
   a. High correlation between the response variable and predictors
   b. High correlation among predictor variables
   c. High variance of the response variable
   d. Lack of correlation between predictors

5. Which criterion balances the goodness of fit and model complexity?
   a. Sum of Squared Residuals (SSR)
   b. Standard error of the estimate (SEE)
   c. Akaike Information Criterion (AIC)
   d. Adjusted R-squared

6. What does a VIF value of 10 or more generally indicate?
   a. Minimal correlation among predictors
   b. Moderate multicollinearity
   c. High multicollinearity
   d. No multicollinearity

7. Which technique is used to evaluate model fit in regression analysis?
   a. Principal component analysis (PCA)
   b. Analysis of Variance (ANOVA)
   c. Sum of Squared Residuals (SSR)
   d. Cluster analysis

8. What does the Akaike Information Criterion (AIC) help in selecting?
   a. The best predictor variable
   b. The best transformation for data
   c. The most parsimonious model
   d. The most complex model

9. Which plot is most commonly used to check the assumptions of linear regression models?
   a. Q-Q plot
   b. Scatter plot
   c. Histogram
   d. Box plot

10. In logistic regression, what does the regression coefficient represent?
    a. Change in the expected log odds of the outcome for a one-unit change in the predictor
    b. Change in the predicted value for a one-unit change in the predictor
    c. Change in the mean of the outcome variable
    d. Change in the residual variance for a one-unit change in the predictor

Long Answer Questions

1. Explain how to apply multiple linear regression analysis to a dataset with multiple predictors. Describe the steps involved in model building, including how to handle multicollinearity and interpret the regression coefficients.
2. Analyze a given dataset using multiple logistic regression. Discuss the importance of adjusting for confounding variables and explain how to interpret the adjusted odds ratios. Provide a detailed example including how you would use statistical software for this analysis.
3. Describe the concept of multicollinearity and its impact on regression analysis. Explain how Variance Inflation Factors (VIFs) are used to detect multicollinearity and interpret different VIF values.
4. Given a set of actual and predicted values, compute the Sum of Squared Residuals (SSR), standard error of the estimate (SEE), and Akaike Information Criterion (AIC). Discuss how these metrics can be used to evaluate model fit.
5. Compare and contrast simple linear regression (SLR) with multiple linear regression (MLR). Discuss the scenarios where each model is appropriate, and explain how you would interpret the results of an MLR model when including interaction terms.
6. Explain the concept of the Akaike Information Criterion (AIC) and its role in model selection. Discuss how AIC balances model goodness of fit with model complexity and why this balance is important.
7. Given two sets of rankings from two different coaches, use Kendall's Tau to assess the agreement between the rankings. Describe the process of calculating Kendall's Tau and interpret the results.
8. Demonstrate how to perform a diagnostic check for multicollinearity in a multiple regression model. Use a practical example to illustrate how to calculate and interpret the Variance Inflation Factors (VIFs) and discuss potential remedies if high multicollinearity is detected.

Solution to MCQs

1. R-squared
2. High multicollinearity
3. T-test
4. High correlation among predictor variables
5. Akaike Information Criterion (AIC)
6. High multicollinearity
7. Sum of Squared Residuals (SSR)
8. The most parsimonious model
9. Q-Q plot
10. Change in the expected log odds of the outcome for a one-unit change in the predictor

Time Series Analysis

5

Time Series Analysis

Introduction to Time Series, Time Series Objects, Trends and Seasonality Variation, Decomposition of Time Series, Seasonal Models, Smoothing and Decomposition, Autocorrelation, Partial Autocorrelation, Interpretation of ACF and PACF, Correlation, Exponential Smoothing, Holt-Winters Method

5.1   Introduction to Time Series

A time series is a set of data points collected or recorded over time, usually at equal intervals. This type of data is commonly used in a range of fields, including finance, economics, and environmental research. Each data point in a time series represents a measurement or observation made at a specific time, and the primary goal is to analyze the sequence to gain a better understanding of the underlying structure and behavior over time. The research can reveal patterns such as trends, seasonal effects, and cyclic behaviors, all of which are required for making sound decisions. For example, in finance, examining historical stock prices can help investors recognize market trends and make strategic investment decisions.

Time series analysis employs a number of tools and procedures to extract relevant statistics and features from data. These methods include descriptive techniques like data charting to show patterns and seasonal variations, as well as more advanced statistical methods like Autoregressive Integrated Moving Average (ARIMA) models and machine learning approaches like Long Short-Term Memory (LSTM) networks. Time series forecasting, a key component of time series analysis, uses these models to estimate future values based on previously observed data. Accurate forecasting is essential for planning and decision-making in a wide range of applications, including anticipating economic indicators, forecasting weather

© Ramchandra S Mangrulkar and Pallavi Vijay Chavan 2025
R. S. Mangrulkar and P. Vijay Chavan, *Predictive Analytics with SAS and R*,
https://doi.org/10.1007/979-8-8688-0905-7_5

patterns, and managing inventory in businesses. Analysts and researchers can produce more precise and trustworthy projections if they understand and apply the aspects of time series.

5.2   Time Series Objects

Time series data structures are critical for managing and analyzing data points accumulated over time. These specialized objects manage time-stamped data in an efficient manner, allowing time-related actions to run smoothly. They are widely supported in a variety of programming languages and statistical software packages, providing particular capabilities for storing, manipulating, and evaluating time-related datasets.

5.2.1   Key Features of Time Series Objects

Key features of time series objects include timestamps, observations, frequency, trend, seasonality, noise, stationarity, autocorrelation, forecasting, and visualization as given below:

- **Indexing:** Time series objects use time-based indexing, which allows for easy extraction and manipulation of data points based on their timestamps. This is crucial for aligning data points accurately in time.
- **Frequency and periodicity:** Time series objects can handle different frequencies (e.g., daily, monthly, quarterly) and periodicity, enabling the analysis of data collected at various intervals.
- **Missing values handling:** Time series objects may manage a variety of frequencies and periodicities (e.g., daily, monthly, quarterly), allowing for the analysis of data acquired at varied intervals.
- **Time zone awareness:** Many time series objects are aware of time zones, which is critical for data collected from multiple geographic regions.
- **Integration with statistical methods:** Time series objects are frequently used with statistical and machine learning techniques, allowing for decomposition, smoothing, and forecasting directly within the data structure.

5.2.2   Types of Time Series Objects

We'll now go over three sorts of objects that are commonly used to store and analyze time series data:

- **The `data.frame`** (in base R)
- **The `ts` object** (in base R)
- **The `xts` object** (created through the `xts` library)

We look into the structures of these goods, as well as their strengths and limits. In the following chapter, we will also discuss the various techniques to visualizing them.

5.2.3 Characteristics of Time Series Data

Characteristics of time series data include sequential observations over time, often exhibiting trends, seasonality, and irregular fluctuations. Some of them are described as follows:

a. **Temporal ordering:** Time series data is organized chronologically, with each observation denoted by time periods such as minutes, hours, days, months, or years.
b. **Trend:** Time series frequently show long-term directionality, indicating whether the data is rising, decreasing, or steady over time. Trends may be linear, exponential, or cyclic.
c. **Seasonality:** Many time series data show regular patterns or changes with a definite frequency, such as daily, weekly, monthly, or annual cycles. These trends are known as seasonality.
d. **Random variation:** Time series data frequently contain random fluctuations or noise, which indicate short-term variations that are unpredictable and cannot be explained by trend or seasonality.

5.2.4 Key Concepts in Time Series Analysis

Key concepts in time series analysis include stationarity, autocorrelation, time series decomposition, forecasting methods (such as ARIMA and exponential smoothing), spectral analysis, and modeling seasonal patterns and trends. Some of them are described as follows:

a. **Descriptive analysis:** Initially, time series data is visually examined to detect trends, patterns, and abnormalities. Descriptive statistics, such as mean, median, variance, and standard deviation, are used to summarize data.
b. **Autocorrelation and partial autocorrelation:** Autocorrelation evaluates the relationship between a time series and a lagged version of itself at various time intervals. Partial autocorrelation calculates the correlation between a time series and its lagged variants after adjusting for intermediate delays.
c. **Forecasting:** Time series analysis forecasts future values using previous data and statistical models. Forecast accuracy is measured using measures such as mean absolute error (MAE), mean squared error (MSE), and root mean squared error (RMSE).

5.2.5   Applications of Time Series Analysis

Applications of time series analysis span various domains, including finance (for stock market predictions), economics (for GDP forecasting), weather forecasting, epidemiology (for disease outbreak patterns), engineering (for predictive maintenance), and even social sciences (for analyzing trends in public opinion). Few applications are

a. **Economics and finance:** Time series analysis is extensively used in economic forecasting, stock market prediction, and modeling economic indicators such as GDP, inflation rates, and unemployment.
b. **Weather forecasting:** Meteorologists use time series analysis to forecast weather conditions, including temperature, precipitation, wind speed, and humidity, based on historical weather data.
c. **Signal processing:** Time series analysis is applied in signal processing for analyzing and filtering signals in various domains such as audio processing, image processing, and telecommunications.
d. **Healthcare:** In healthcare, time series analysis is used for monitoring patient vital signs, analyzing medical sensor data, predicting disease outbreaks, and modeling epidemiological trends.

5.3   Trends and Seasonality Variation

Trends and seasonality are two key components of time series data, describing predictable patterns and oscillations throughout time. Understanding and modeling trends and seasonality variation is critical for gaining useful insights, creating accurate forecasts, and identifying underlying dynamics in time series data.

5.3.1   Trends

A trend is the long-term direction or general pattern observed in a time series over a lengthy period. Trends can appear in a variety of ways:

a. **Upward trend:** In an ascending trend, the data points show a constant growth over time. This might signify an increase, expansion, or improvement in the underlying process being measured.
b. **Downward trend:** In contrast, a negative trend indicates a continuous decline in data points over time. This might indicate a decrease, contraction, or degradation in the process being monitored.
c. **Flat trend:** A flat trend happens when the data points do not change considerably over time, suggesting that the underlying mechanism is stable or at equilibrium.

Identifying and modeling trends is critical for comprehending the underlying dynamics of a time series and making sound decisions. Trend analysis sometimes entails fitting mathematical models to data, such as linear regression or exponential smoothing, in order to quantify the trend component and distinguish it from other causes of variation.

5.3.2   Seasonality

Seasonality is defined as the repeated, periodic variations observed in a time series at regular periods. These oscillations are often caused by regular external causes like weather, holidays, or business cycles. Seasonality has several key aspects, including

a. **Fixed periodicity:** Seasonal patterns occur at regular intervals, such as daily, weekly, monthly, or annual cycles. For example, retail sales may peak during holiday seasons or weekends.
b. **Consistent amplitude:** Seasonal changes frequently have a consistent magnitude or amplitude throughout cycles. However, the particular amplitude may differ based on customer behavior, economic situations, or marketing methods.
c. **Seasonal adjustment:** Seasonality can hide underlying trends, making it difficult to identify long-term patterns. Seasonal adjustment strategies, such as seasonal decomposition or X-12-ARIMA models, are used to eliminate seasonal influences and separate the underlying trend and irregular components.

Analyzing and modeling seasonality variance is critical for effective forecasting and decision-making, especially in businesses impacted by seasonal demand or supply swings. Understanding seasonal trends allows firms to optimize inventory management, production scheduling, and marketing tactics to capitalize on seasonal peaks while mitigating seasonal downturns.

5.3.2.1 Interaction Between Trends and Seasonality
Trends and seasonality frequently interact in time series data, with seasonal variations overlaying the underlying trend. For example, an upward trend in retail sales might be boosted by seasonal surges over the holiday season. Understanding the relationship between trends and seasonality is crucial for creating reliable forecasting models that take into consideration both long-term trends and periodic changes. In conclusion, trends and seasonality variation are critical components of time series data that impact decision-making and forecasting across several domains. By finding, analyzing, and modeling trends and seasonality, analysts may acquire useful insights, make accurate forecasts, and get a better grasp of the underlying dynamics driving temporal data patterns.

5.4   Decomposition of Time Series

Decomposition of time series is a key approach in time series analysis that aims to disentangle the numerous components that contribute to the overall pattern observed in a time series dataset. By breaking down a time series into its constituent elements, analysts can gain a better understanding of the underlying structure, spot trends, seasonal patterns, and irregular variations and generate more accurate projections.

5.4.1   Components of Time Series Decomposition

Components of time series decomposition typically include trend, seasonality, and residual (or noise) components.

a. **Trend component:** The trend component depicts the long-term movement or directionality of the data series. It measures the underlying increase or drop in the data over time, disregarding short-term variations. Trends can be linear, suggesting a consistent pace of change, or nonlinear, with more complicated patterns.
b. **Seasonal component:** The seasonal component captures repeating patterns or variations that occur at regular intervals across the time period. These patterns frequently correspond to seasonal fluctuations caused by external variables such as weather, holidays, or economic cycles. Seasonal variations often have a constant magnitude and frequency throughout numerous cycles.
c. **Irregular component (residual):** The irregular component, also known as the residual component, reflects random fluctuation or noise in the data that cannot be explained by the trend or seasonal patterns. It includes unforeseeable fluctuations, measurement mistakes, and unmodeled elements that influence the time series.

5.4.2   Methods of Time Series Decomposition

Methods of time series decomposition include classical decomposition, STL (seasonal and trend decomposition using LOESS), X-13-ARIMA-SEATS, and wavelet decomposition. In broad sense, we can have the following decompositions:

a. **Classical decomposition:** Classical decomposition approaches, such as additive and multiplicative decomposition models, use mathematical techniques such as moving averages or regression analysis to divide a time series into trend, seasonal, and irregular components. In the additive model, the components are added together, but in the multiplicative model, they are multiplied.
b. **Seasonal decomposition of time series (STL):** The seasonal decomposition of time series (STL) algorithm is a stable and adaptable approach for decomposing

time series data into trend, seasonal, and residual components using a process known as LOESS smoothing. STL can detect and handle non-constant seasonal patterns, and it is especially useful for time series with irregular or nonlinear trends.

c. **Wavelet decomposition:** Wavelet decomposition is a signal processing method that divides time series data into multiple frequency components via wavelet transformations. It enables the discovery of localized patterns and variations at various scales, revealing both short-term and long-term dynamics within the time series.

5.4.3   Applications of Time Series Decomposition

Applications of time series decomposition include seasonal adjustment of economic indicators, trend analysis in climate data, anomaly detection in sensor data, and forecasting sales trends in retail. A few prominent applications are

a. **Forecasting:** Decomposing a time series into trend, seasonal, and irregular components allows analysts to build more accurate forecasting models by modeling each component independently and then combining them to create projections.
b. **Anomaly detection:** Decomposition methods can assist in uncovering anomalous behavior or outliers in data by extracting the irregular component, which indicates departures from the anticipated pattern caused by uncommon occurrences or mistakes.
c. **Seasonal adjustment:** Decomposing a time series removes seasonal impacts from the data, allowing for a more in-depth analysis of underlying trends and irregular variations without the influence of seasonal patterns.

5.5   Time Series with Deterministic Components

Real-world time series usually feature deterministic trends, cyclical patterns, seasonal components, as well as an irregular (stationary process) component. As given in Figure 5-1, the components are

- **Trend component:** This indicates a long-term increase or reduction in data that may not be linear. The trend may change direction over time.
- **Cyclical component:** Data may show spikes and decreases that may not follow a set period. These cycles typically last longer than seasonal patterns. In practice, the cyclical component is frequently combined with the trend component, and the two are referred to as the trend cycle.
- **Seasonal component:** This occurs when the series exhibits seasonal fluctuations (e.g., monthly, quarterly, yearly). Seasonality has a definite and predictable timeframe.
- **Irregular component:** This represents the series' stationary process component.

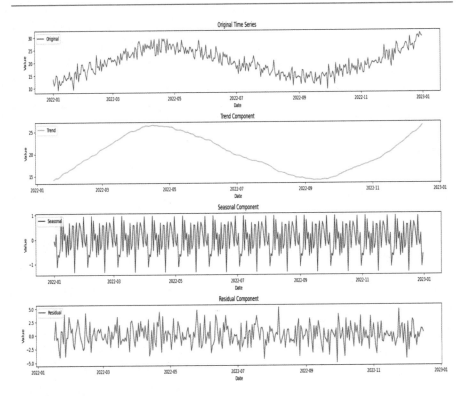

Figure 5-1. Time series components

The following code demonstrates these components in Python:

```
1  import numpy as np
2  import pandas as pd
3  import matplotlib.pyplot as plt
4
5  # Set the seed for reproducibility
6  np.random.seed(0)
7
8  # Generate time series length
9  time = np.arange(100)
10
11 # Trend component (linear for simplicity)
12 trend = 0.1 * time
13
14 # Seasonal component (sinusoidal with a period of 20)
15 seasonal = 10 * np.sin(2 * np.pi * time / 20)
16
17 # Cyclical component (sinusoidal with a period of 50)
18 cyclical = 5 * np.sin(2 * np.pi * time / 50)
19
```

```
20 # Irregular component (random noise)
21 irregular = np.random.normal(0, 1, len(time))
22
23 # Combine all components to create the final time series
24 time_series = trend + seasonal + cyclical + irregular
25
26 # Create a DataFrame for better plotting
27 data = pd.DataFrame({
28     'Time': time,
29     'Trend': trend,
30     'Seasonal': seasonal,
31     'Cyclical': cyclical,
32     'Irregular': irregular,
33     'Time Series': time_series
34 })
35
36 # Plot each component and the combined time series
37 plt.figure(figsize=(14, 10))
38
39 plt.subplot(5, 1, 1)
40 plt.plot(data['Time'], data['Trend'], label='Trend')
41 plt.legend(loc='upper left')
42 plt.title('Trend Component')
43
44 plt.subplot(5, 1, 2)
45 plt.plot(data['Time'], data['Seasonal'], label='Seasonal')
46 plt.legend(loc='upper left')
47 plt.title('Seasonal Component')
48
49 plt.subplot(5, 1, 3)
50 plt.plot(data['Time'], data['Cyclical'], label='Cyclical')
51 plt.legend(loc='upper left')
52 plt.title('Cyclical Component')
53
54 plt.subplot(5, 1, 4)
55 plt.plot(data['Time'], data['Irregular'], label='Irregular')
56 plt.legend(loc='upper left')
57 plt.title('Irregular Component')
58
59 plt.subplot(5, 1, 5)
60 plt.plot(data['Time'], data['Time Series'], label='Time
       Series')
61 plt.legend(loc='upper left')
62 plt.title('Combined Time Series')
63
64 plt.tight_layout()
65 plt.show()
```

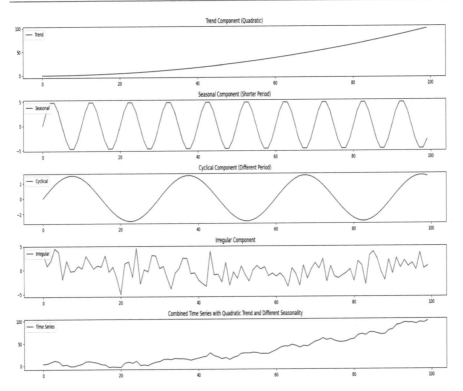

Figure 5-2. Time series components

The output can be summarized in Figure 5-2.

5.6   Trends and Seasonality Variation

The Python code shows how trends and seasonality can change within a time series by creating a synthetic dataset with a quadratic trend and various seasonal patterns. The trend component, defined as $0.01 \times time^2$, is a long-term increase that follows a curved, upward trajectory, unlike a simple linear trend. The seasonal component is shown as a sinusoidal curve with a period of ten, showing that regular fluctuations occur more frequently. Furthermore, the cyclical component, another sinusoidal function with a longer period of 30, introduces longer-term oscillations distinct from the shorter seasonal cycles. To increase realism, an irregular component made up of random noise with greater fluctuation is introduced.

These components are merged to create the final time series, which is shown with Matplotlib subplots. Each subplot shows a separate component, providing for a better understanding of how trends and seasonal changes affect the overall structure of the time series.

The following code demonstrates trends and seasonality variation:

```python
import numpy as np
import pandas as pd
import matplotlib.pyplot as plt

# Set the seed for reproducibility
np.random.seed(0)

# Generate time series length
time = np.arange(100)

# Trend component (quadratic for variation)
trend = 0.01 * time**2

# Seasonal component (sinusoidal with a period of 10 for
    variation)
seasonal = 5 * np.sin(2 * np.pi * time / 10)

# Cyclical component (sinusoidal with a period of 30 for
    variation)
cyclical = 3 * np.sin(2 * np.pi * time / 30)

# Irregular component (random noise)
irregular = np.random.normal(0, 2, len(time))

# Combine all components to create the final time series
time_series = trend + seasonal + cyclical + irregular

# Create a DataFrame for better plotting
data = pd.DataFrame({
    'Time': time,
    'Trend': trend,
    'Seasonal': seasonal,
    'Cyclical': cyclical,
    'Irregular': irregular,
    'Time Series': time_series
})

# Plot each component and the combined time series
plt.figure(figsize=(14, 10))

plt.subplot(5, 1, 1)
plt.plot(data['Time'], data['Trend'], label='Trend')
plt.legend(loc='upper left')
plt.title('Trend Component (Quadratic)')

plt.subplot(5, 1, 2)
plt.plot(data['Time'], data['Seasonal'], label='Seasonal')
plt.legend(loc='upper left')
plt.title('Seasonal Component (Shorter Period)')

plt.subplot(5, 1, 3)
```

```
50 plt.plot(data['Time'], data['Cyclical'], label='Cyclical')
51 plt.legend(loc='upper left')
52 plt.title('Cyclical Component (Different Period)')
53
54 plt.subplot(5, 1, 4)
55 plt.plot(data['Time'], data['Irregular'], label='Irregular')
56 plt.legend(loc='upper left')
57 plt.title('Irregular Component')
58
59 plt.subplot(5, 1, 5)
60 plt.plot(data['Time'], data['Time Series'], label='Time
      Series')
61 plt.legend(loc='upper left')
62 plt.title('Combined Time Series with Quadratic Trend and
      Different Seasonality')
63
64 plt.tight_layout()
65 plt.show()
```

The provided Python code generates and visualizes a synthetic time series with various components: a quadratic trend, a shorter-period seasonal component, a different-period cyclical component, and an irregular component. First, it sets the seed for reproducibility and creates an array representing the time steps. It then defines each component: the quadratic trend component as $0.01 \times \text{time}^2$, the seasonal component as a sinusoidal function with a period of 10, the cyclical component as another sinusoidal function with a period of 30, and the irregular component as random noise with higher variability. The final time series is constructed by combining all these components. The data is stored in a Pandas DataFrame for easy plotting. Finally, the code uses Matplotlib to create subplots for each individual component and the combined time series, providing a clear visualization of how each part contributes to the overall data structure.

5.7   Seasonal Models

In time series analysis, seasonal models are useful tools, especially when working with data that displays periodic patterns like weekly, monthly, annual, or daily cycles. These models are intended to precisely detect and predict these seasonal fluctuations, offering insightful information to a range of sectors, such as manufacturing, retail, and finance.

5.7.1   Recognizing Seasonal Patterns

Understanding seasonal patterns in time series data is essential before diving into seasonal models. Seasonal patterns are regular oscillations or variations that take place at predetermined intervals within a given period of time. Numerous things, including the weather, holidays, cultural events, and economic cycles, can have an impact on these patterns. Take sales data from a retail business, for instance. Holiday seasons like Christmas and Thanksgiving may see sales peaks and troughs throughout the year. Businesses must comprehend these seasonal patterns and appropriately model them in order to maximize personnel numbers, marketing campaigns, and inventory management.

5.7.2 Seasonal Decomposition of Time Series (STL)

The STL method is a popular method for examining seasonal patterns. A time series is broken down by STL into three primary parts: residual, trend, and seasonal.

Seasonal component: The data's recurring patterns or seasonality are captured by this component. It is a representation of the periodic, systematic fluctuations. Depending on whether the size of the fluctuations stays constant or changes in proportion to the series level, seasonal patterns can be either additive or multiplicative.

Trend component: The long-term movement or direction of the time series data is measured by the trend component. It helps identify if the trend in the data is rising, dropping, or both over time. Depending on the type of data, trends can be polynomial, exponential, or linear.

5.7.3 STL Algorithm

The following steps are involved in the STL algorithm:

1. To divide the time series data into seasonal, trend, and residual components, apply a robust filtering strategy.
2. Adjust residual, trend, and seasonal models in relation to the disassembled parts.
3. To show the size of seasonal variations at each time point, compute seasonal indices.
4. Reconstruct the initial time series data by combining the seasonal, trend, and residual components.

5.7.4 Visualization and Interpretation

Visualizing the decomposed components of the time series data might yield significant insights into its underlying patterns. Let's look at a retail store's monthly sales data example given in Figure 5-3.

Original data: A time-plot of the unprocessed sales data.

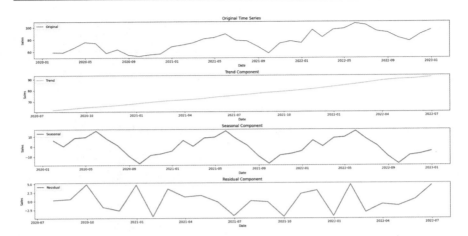

Figure 5-3. Retail store's monthly sales data

Seasonal component: The variations in sales that correspond with the seasons, emphasizing regular patterns like holiday season peaks.

Trend component: The trend component of sales is their long-term tendency, which indicates whether they are increasing, decreasing, or remaining constant over time.

Residual component: The noise or erratic swings in sales data that are not explained by seasonal and trend components are known as the residual component.

Time series data with recurrent patterns can be effectively analyzed and forecasted using seasonal models, like STL. Through the use of seasonal, trend, and residual data components, these models help analysts identify underlying trends, produce precise projections, and derive useful information for making decisions. Seasonal models are essential for streamlining operations and promoting corporate expansion in a variety of industries, including retail and finance.

5.8   Smoothing and Decomposition

Time series data frequently show trends, seasonal patterns, and noise in different forms, which can mask underlying patterns and complicate forecasting. In time series analysis, smoothing and decomposition techniques are critical instruments for obtaining significant insights, recognizing patterns, and producing precise forecasts. This part covers smoothing and decomposition techniques.

5.8.1 Smoothing Techniques

In time series data, smoothing techniques seek to eliminate noise and reveal underlying patterns. These methods entail averaging or combining data points over a predetermined time frame. Moving averages and exponential smoothing are two popular methods of smoothing.

Moving averages: By averaging the data points that are adjacent to each other inside a sliding frame, moving averages help to reduce oscillations in time series data. The size of the window or the number of data points utilized in the computation determines how much smoothing is applied. A three-period moving average, for instance, computes the average of the two most recent and current data points. Take daily temperature data as an example. By averaging the temperatures over the previous seven days, a seven-day moving average can be applied to remove daily variations and provide a smoother picture of temperature patterns.

Exponential smoothing: In this method, the weights of earlier observations are exponentially reduced, while the weights of more recent observations are increased. When dealing with time series data that exhibit seasonality or shifting trends, this technique is quite helpful. The simplest type of exponential smoothing is called simple exponential smoothing (SES), and it regulates the rate of decay with just one smoothing parameter, alpha. Let's say we have monthly sales information for a retail establishment. We can create projections by gradually diminishing the influence of older observations and giving greater weight to recent sales data through the use of exponential smoothing.

5.8.2 Decomposition Techniques

In time series analysis, decomposition techniques divide data into discrete elements like trend, seasonality, and residual, which help uncover underlying patterns and produce precise forecasts. These methods, which include STL and classical decomposition, provide significant new insights into the dynamics and composition of time series data. Decomposition techniques can be used to separate time series data into trend, seasonal, and residual components. This dissection facilitates predictions and helps to clarify the underlying trends.

1. **Seasonal decomposition of time series (STL):** A time series is broken down into three primary parts using STL – residual, trend, and seasonal. To distinguish between various elements and offer insights into irregular fluctuations, long-term trends, and seasonal patterns, it employs strong filtering algorithms. For instance, using STL decomposition to analyze monthly airline passenger data might reveal residual noise, long-term trends showing an increase or decrease in passenger traffic, and seasonal changes related to vacation seasons.
2. **Classical decomposition (additive and multiplicative):** A time series can be divided into additive or multiplicative components using classical decomposi-

tion. The seasonal and trend components are assumed to fluctuate proportionately with the series level in multiplicative decomposition, but to have a fixed amount in additive decomposition.

Example: Using additive decomposition to break down quarterly GDP data can show consistent seasonal changes between quarters, whereas using multiplicative decomposition can show that seasonal patterns intensify as GDP rises.

Forecasting retail sales is one application of smoothing and decomposition algorithms in real life. Retailers frequently examine past sales information to forecast demand, enhance inventory control, and develop marketing plans. Retailers can uncover underlying trends and eliminate noise from sales data by using smoothing techniques like exponential smoothing. For example, retailers might create projections by smoothing out short-term variances and giving more weight to recent sales data using simple exponential smoothing (SES). Retail sales analysis also makes extensive use of decomposition techniques like seasonal decomposition of time series (STL). Retailers can understand seasonal patterns (e.g., peak sales around holidays), long-term trends (e.g., growing or declining sales over time), and irregular variations by breaking down sales data into seasonal, trend, and residual components. In order for retailers to stay competitive in ever-changing markets and to gain useful insights from past data, they need to employ smoothing and decomposition techniques in their retail sales forecasting. Retailers may foster corporate success, improve customer pleasure, and streamline operations by proficiently evaluating and interpreting sales data.

5.9   Autocorrelation

Autocorrelation: unveiling temporal dependencies
Time series analysis relies heavily on autocorrelation, which is essential for comprehending the complex interactions between historical and prospective observations in a given dataset. It explores the innate connections between a variable's past values and its future states, illuminating patterns, trends, and dependencies that are essential for predicting modeling and making decisions in a variety of contexts. This thorough examination delves deeper into autocorrelation, covering everything from its theoretical underpinnings to its real-world applications. It is enhanced with instructive examples, graphical representations, methods, and use cases.

Understanding autocorrelation
The degree to which a time series correlates with its lagged variants can be ascertained by autocorrelation, commonly referred to as serial correlation. It measures how closely observations at various time intervals correlate or are similar to one another. While negative autocorrelation suggests an inverse link, positive autocorrelation indicates that past values influence future ones in the same manner. There appears to be no visible association between past and future data when the autocorrelation is zero. For example, take into consideration a retail store's monthly sales dataset. A positive autocorrelation may suggest a positive trend or seasonality, whereby better sales in one month are followed by higher sales in

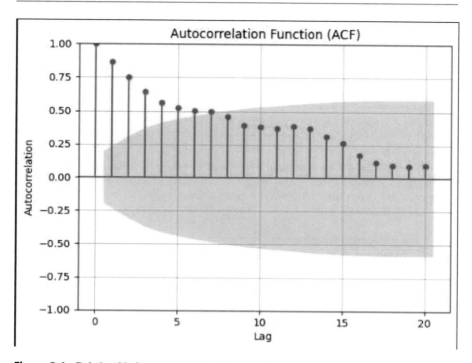

Figure 5-4. Relationship between autocorrelation and lag

subsequent months. On the other hand, negative autocorrelation may indicate a corrective behavior, in which periods with unusually high sales are usually followed by periods with decreased sales.

Figure 5-4 shows the relationship between autocorrelation and lag, which calculates the correlation between observations made at various time delays. The autocorrelation coefficient at each lag, which shows the intensity and direction of the link between data separated by that lag, is shown by a bar or line segment on the figure. Significant autocorrelation at increasing lags shows association across longer time intervals, but substantial autocorrelation at lag 1 indicates a strong linear link between neighboring observations. Understanding the temporal dependence structure in the data is aided by the plot and is essential for a number of time series analytic tasks, including forecasting, pattern recognition, and model selection.

The correlation between time series measurements made at various times in time is referred to as autocorrelation, or serial correlation. Autocorrelation can be broadly classified into two types:

1. Positive autocorrelation

    A time series exhibits positive autocorrelation when there is a positive correlation between consecutive data. According to this, if one data point is greater (or lower) than the mean, then it is likely that the next data point will likewise be higher (or lower) than the mean. A trend or seasonality in the data is frequently indicated by positive autocorrelation. As an illustration, positive autocorrelation in stock prices may imply that, should the price rise today, it will probably do so over the course of the following several days.

2. Negative autocorrelation

Negative autocorrelation is the result of successive observations in a time series having a negative correlation with one another. If the current data point is higher (or lower) than the mean, it suggests that the subsequent data points will most likely be lower (or higher) than the mean.

Negative autocorrelation may be a sign of mean reversion or corrective action in the data. Negative autocorrelation, for example, may suggest that a rise in stock price today raises the probability of a price decrease in the days to follow in the financial markets.

5.9.1 Applications for Autocorrelation

The applications for autocorrelation can be found in several domains:

1. **Time series analysis:** To help predict future values, autocorrelation is necessary to identify patterns and trends in time series data.
2. **Signal processing:** It is employed in signal processing to identify periodicity or recurring patterns by analyzing signals.
3. **Econometrics:** The study of economic time series data, the detection of economic cycles, and the modeling of economic phenomena all depend on autocorrelation analysis.
4. **Quality control:** By identifying departures from expected behavior in sequential data, autocorrelation aids in process monitoring and control.
5. **Climate research:** Autocorrelation is used in climate research to examine long-term trends and variability as well as temporal patterns in climate data, such as temperature or precipitation.

5.9.2 Partial Autocorrelation

A statistical concept called partial autocorrelation is used to calculate the correlation between data in a time series while accounting for the impact of additional observations made at varying intervals. When determining the direct relationship between two time points while accounting for the influence of intermediate time points, it is especially helpful. After accounting for all intermediate data, partial autocorrelation at lag k, or PACF(k), calculates the correlation between two observations in a time series that are k time units apart. To put it another way, it measures the correlation between two points in time while accounting for the impact of the time points in between.

Steps:

1. **Calculate autocorrelation:** Determine the autocorrelation function (ACF) of the time series data up to lag k first. This step involves calculating the correlation coefficient between the original time series and lag-adjusted versions of itself at various time lags.
2. **Multiple regression:** Use all prior observations up to lag k as predictor variables in multiple linear regression to forecast each observation in the time series. The coefficients of determination, or R-squared values, are computed for each regression after each observation is regressed on its lag values.
3. **Partial autocorrelation:** The partial autocorrelation at lag k is the coefficient of determination (R-squared) of the regression model divided by the R-squared value of the full regression model at lag k. This model predicts the current observation alone by using lag k as the predictor variable.

Consider the example. Take a look at a monthly sales dataset that spans multiple years. To determine the direct association between sales in subsequent months while adjusting for the influence of any intermediate month, we wish to examine the partial autocorrelation.
Steps:

1. **Calculate autocorrelation:** Determine the sales data's autocorrelation function (ACF) up to lag k, or lag 12 for a year.
2. **Multiple regression:** Regress each observation on its lagged values up to lag k using multiple linear regression. For example, forecast June sales based on June, May, April, and other sales in the past.
3. **Partial autocorrelation:** To calculate the partial autocorrelation at lag k, divide the R-squared of the regression model at lag k (i.e., incorporating all lags up to May) by the R-squared of the regression model utilizing only the lag k predictor (May, for example).

Figure 5-5 shows the partial autocorrelation function (PACF) for a three-year hypothetical monthly sales dataset. The partial autocorrelation coefficient at a given lag is shown by each bar in the plot, which shows the strength and direction of the association between sales in subsequent months while accounting for the impact of interim months. Independent of the impacts of the months in between, a significant partial autocorrelation coefficient at a given lag indicates a direct association between sales at that lag and the current month's sales. For instance, even after taking into consideration any other monthly impacts, a substantial partial autocorrelation coefficient with a lag of one month suggests that sales in the prior month have a considerable influence on sales in the current month. With the use of this graphical depiction, analysts may pinpoint significant lags and add them to time series models for precise forecasting, planning, and decision-making in sales management.

Thus, the impact of intermediate observations is taken into account by partial autocorrelation, which calculates the direct correlation between observations in a time series at particular delays. It facilitates the discovery of temporal connections

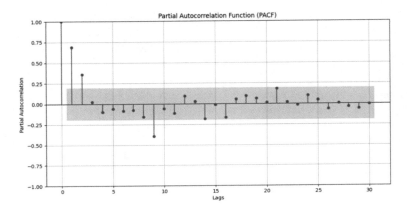

Figure 5-5. Partial autocorrelation function (PACF)

and important lag effects in data. Reliability between observations at specific lags is indicated by significant partial autocorrelation coefficients, which facilitate predictive modeling. Plotting the partial autocorrelation function (PACF) is a graphic way to depict partial autocorrelation.

5.9.3   Interpretation of ACF and PACF

Interpretation of ACF (autocorrelation function) and PACF (partial autocorrelation function) involves identifying patterns of correlation and direct influence, respectively, among lagged values in time series data, crucial for model selection in forecasting and analysis.

Autocorrelation Function (ACF)

ACF calculates the correlation at various lags between a time series and a lagged version of itself. It facilitates the identification of trends, seasonality, and patterns in the data. Significant temporal dependence is indicated by a substantial ACF value at a certain lag. The ACF quantifies the degree of similarity between observations made at various times. Perfect positive correlation is represented by a value of 1, perfect negative correlation is represented by a value of −1, and no correlation is shown by a value of 0. A persistent pattern or trend in the data is shown by a strong autocorrelation at a particular delay.

Steps to calculate ACF:

1. Up to a given lag, calculate the covariance between the time series and its lag variants.
2. To obtain autocorrelation coefficients, normalize the covariances.
3. Plot the associated lags against the autocorrelation coefficients.

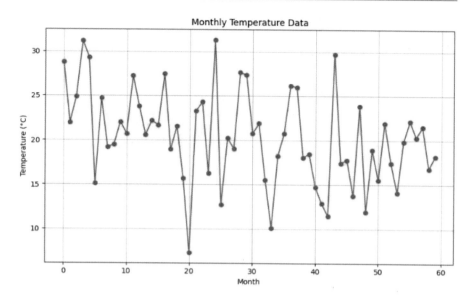

Figure 5-6. Dataset with monthly temperature data

Let us examine a monthly temperature record spanning multiple years for a certain city. The average temperature for a month is represented by each observation. To determine the extent of connection between the temperature readings at various time lags, we wish to examine the ACF.

The ACF plot displays the autocorrelation coefficient on the y-axis and the lag (measured in months) on the x-axis as given in Figure 5-6. The ACF plot's notable peaks and troughs show whether the data contain temporal cycles or patterns. If, for instance, a notable peak appears at a 12-month (1-year) lag, this may indicate annual seasonality in the temperature data, meaning that historical temperatures for a certain month are typically connected with current temperatures.

Time series forecasting and modeling require an understanding of the underlying temporal dependencies present in the time series data, which can be obtained by examining the ACF plot.

Analyzing the Autocorrelation Function (ACF) and Partial Autocorrelation Function (PACF) for the example provided offers insights into the temporal relationships within the data. It records correlations between observations, both direct and indirect. Every bar in the PACF figure denotes the partial autocorrelation coefficient at a particular lag. It eliminates the impact of intermediate lags by isolating direct relationships. We can also compare ACF and PACF as given in Table 5-1.

Table 5-1. Comparison of ACF and PACF

ACF (Autocorrelation Function)	PACF (Partial Autocorrelation Function)
1. Plots using ACF labels are useful for spotting temporal connections in data	1. Plots using PACF labels are useful for spotting temporal connections in data
2. ACF captures both indirect and direct relationships	2. PACF isolates direct connections
3. Peaks in ACF may become less pronounced or vanish in PACF if there are indirect linkages	3. Peaks in PACF indicate direct correlations, which match significant values in ACF
4. Significant spikes in ACF show both direct and indirect correlations	4. Significant spikes in PACF show direct correlations

5.10   Exponential Smoothing

Time series forecasting is crucial in many disciplines, including supply chain management, marketing, economics, finance, and economics. The main objective of time series forecasting is to predict future values based on past observations, enabling organizations to plan ahead and make informed decisions. Two well-liked time series forecasting techniques that are well liked for their versatility, effectiveness, and simplicity are the Holt-Winters method and exponential smoothing. In this chapter, we examine these methods in detail, exposing their underlying concepts, mathematical formulations, and practical applications.

5.10.1 Basic Exponential Smoothing

Based on the idea of weighted averaging, simple exponential smoothing is a crucial method in time series forecasting. Essentially, the approach gives historical observations exponentially decreasing weights, i.e., more recent observations are given a higher weight than earlier ones. The prediction for the future period, shown as F_{t+1}, is computed as a combination of the current observation and the prior forecast, while the level component, represented as L_t, displays the current estimate of the time series' level. The graph in Figure 5-7 gives basic exponential smoothing.

The basic exponential smoothing mathematical expression is as follows:

$$F_{t+1} = \alpha \times Y_t + (1 - \alpha) \times F_t \tag{5-1}$$

$$L_{t+1} = \alpha \times Y_t + (1 - \alpha) \times L_t \tag{5-2}$$

where

- F_{t+1} is the forecast for the next period.
- Y_t is the observation for the current period.

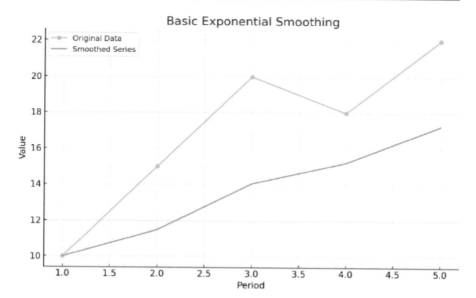

Figure 5-7. Basic exponential smoothing

- F_t is the forecast for the current period.
- L_t is the level estimate for the current period.
- α is the smoothing parameter, often referred to as the smoothing factor or smoothing coefficient, with $0 \leq \alpha \leq 1$.

The smoothing parameter α controls how quickly past observations affect the future. When the alpha value is higher, the forecast is more responsive to variations in the data because it gives more weight to recent observations. Conversely, because it assigns more equal weights to earlier observations, a forecast with a smaller alpha value is smoother and less susceptible to short-term fluctuations.

The Python code with proper indentation, formatting, and fixed issues for visualizing the process of basic exponential smoothing using the given time series dataset:

```
import matplotlib.pyplot as plt

# Example time series data
periods = [1, 2, 3, 4, 5]
observations = [10, 15, 20, 18, 22]

# Initialize smoothed series with the first observation
smoothed_series = [observations[0]]

# Smoothing parameter
alpha = 0.3
```

```
12
13  # Perform exponential smoothing
14  for i in range(1, len(observations)):
15      smoothed_value = alpha * observations[i] + (1 - alpha) *
        smoothed_series[i-1]
16      smoothed_series.append(smoothed_value)
17
18  # Plot original data and smoothed series
19  plt.figure(figsize=(10, 6))
20  plt.plot(periods, observations, marker='o', label='Original
        Data')
21  plt.plot(periods, smoothed_series, marker='x', label='
        Smoothed Series')
22  plt.title('Basic Exponential Smoothing')
23  plt.xlabel('Period')
24  plt.ylabel('Value')
25  plt.legend()
26  plt.grid(True)
27  plt.show()
```

The graph illustrates the smoothing process, with the smoothed series gradually converging toward the observed values while dampening short-term fluctuations. This approach allows for the extraction of underlying trends and patterns from noisy data, facilitating more accurate forecasting.

5.10.2 Single Exponential Smoothing

Single exponential smoothing, a special case of basic exponential smoothing, simplifies the method by utilizing only one smoothing parameter (α). This technique is particularly useful for datasets with no discernible trend or seasonality, where the focus is primarily on smoothing out noise and generating short-term forecasts.

The mathematical formulation for single exponential smoothing is identical to that of basic exponential smoothing, with the level estimate L_t and forecast F_{t+1} calculated using the same equations. However, in single exponential smoothing, there's no separate trend component, making it more straightforward to implement and interpret.

```
1   import matplotlib.pyplot as plt
2
3   # Example time series data
4   periods = [1, 2, 3, 4, 5, 6, 7, 8, 9, 10]
5   observations = [10, 15, 20, 18, 22, 25, 28, 30, 35, 40]
6
7   # Initialize smoothed series with the first observation
8   smoothed_series = [observations[0]]
9
10  # Smoothing parameter
11  alpha = 0.3
12
```

```
13 # Perform single exponential smoothing
14 for i in range(1, len(observations)):
15     smoothed_value = alpha * observations[i] + (1 - alpha) *
       smoothed_series[i-1]
16     smoothed_series.append(smoothed_value)
17
18 # Plot original data and smoothed series
19 plt.figure(figsize=(10, 6))
20 plt.plot(periods, observations, marker='o', label='Original
   Data')
21 plt.plot(periods, smoothed_series, marker='x', label='
   Smoothed Series')
22 plt.title('Single Exponential Smoothing')
23 plt.xlabel('Period')
24 plt.ylabel('Value')
25 plt.legend()
26 plt.grid(True)
27 plt.show()
```

Graphs in Figure 5-8 show single exponential smoothing, whereas the basic exponential smoothing is given in Figure 5-7, demonstrating that both strategies result in the same smoothed series. Single exponential smoothing produces a more responsive forecast as it does not include a trend component, allowing for faster response to data changes. The Holt-Winters method, also known as triple exponential smoothing, adds seasonality to the forecasting process, building on Holt's work.

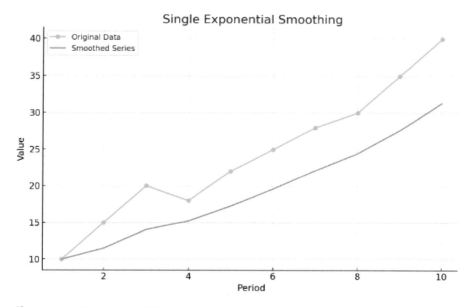

Figure 5-8. Single exponential smoothing

5.11   Holt-Winters Method

Time series data often exhibit three main components:

- **Level** (L_t): The average value of the series over time
- **Trend** (T_t): The direction and rate of change in the series over time
- **Seasonality** (S_t): Periodic fluctuations or patterns that repeat at regular intervals

The Holt-Winters method combines these components to produce forecasts that account for both the underlying trend and seasonal variations in the data as given in Figure 5-9.

The Holt-Winters method involves three sets of equations to update the level, trend, and seasonal components iteratively. Let's denote the following.

The forecast F_{t+m} is calculated as the sum of the level, trend, and seasonal components:

$$F_{t+m} = (L_t + m \times T_t) \times S_{t-m+k}$$

The level L_t and trend T_t estimates are updated using exponential smoothing:

$$L_t = \alpha \times \frac{Y_t}{S_{t-m}} + (1 - \alpha) \times (L_{t-1} + T_{t-1})$$

$$T_t = \beta \times (L_t - L_{t-1}) + (1 - \beta) \times T_{t-1}$$

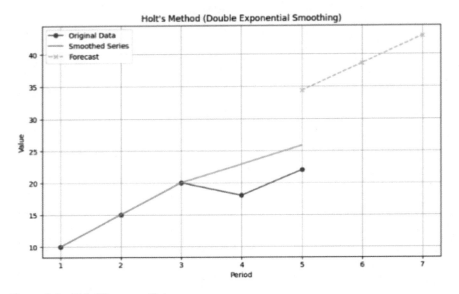

Figure 5-9. Holt-Winters coefficient

The seasonal estimate S_t is updated using a seasonal adjustment factor:

$$S_t = \gamma \times \frac{Y_t}{L_t} + (1 - \gamma) \times S_{t-m}$$

5.11.1 Seasonal Adjustment

One crucial decision in implementing the Holt-Winters method is choosing between additive and multiplicative seasonality:

- **Additive seasonality:** The seasonal component is added to the level.
- **Multiplicative seasonality:** The seasonal component is multiplied by the level.

The choice of multiplicative vs. additive seasonality depends on the kind of seasonal patterns in the data. For instance, multiplicative seasonality might be more appropriate if the seasonal changes' amplitude is consistently proportional to the series' level. On the other hand, if the seasonal fluctuations are more stable in absolute terms, additive seasonality can be preferred.

5.11.2 Forecasting Process

To forecast future values using the Holt-Winters method, the following steps are typically followed: First, initialize the level, trend, and seasonal estimates based on historical data. Next, update the estimates iteratively using the smoothing equations. Finally, forecast future values based on the updated estimates.

5.11.3 Implementation Considerations

When implementing the Holt-Winters method, several factors should be considered:

- **Selection of smoothing parameters α, β, γ:** The choice of smoothing parameters significantly affects the forecasting accuracy. These parameters are typically selected through experimentation or optimization techniques.
- **Handling of seasonality:** Identifying the appropriate type of seasonality (additive vs. multiplicative) and determining the number of seasonal periods are critical steps in implementing the method.
- **Model evaluation:** Assessing the accuracy of forecasts using appropriate error metrics and comparing them against alternative forecasting methods.

```
 1 import numpy as np
 2 import matplotlib.pyplot as plt
 3
 4 def holt_method(series, alpha, beta, periods):
 5     # Initialization
 6     level = series[0]
 7     trend = series[1] - series[0]  # Initial trend estimate
 8     smoothed_series = [series[0]]
 9     forecast = [series[0]]
10
11     # Holt's Method (Double Exponential Smoothing)
12     for i in range(1, len(series) + periods):
13         if i < len(series):
14             observation = series[i]
15         else:
16             observation = forecast[-1]  # Use forecasted
    value for future periods
17
18         # Level and trend updates
19         prev_level = level
20         level = alpha * observation + (1 - alpha) * (level +
    trend)
21         trend = beta * (level - prev_level) + (1 - beta) *
    trend
22
23         # Forecast calculation
24         forecast.append(level + trend)
25         smoothed_series.append(level)
26
27     return smoothed_series, forecast
28
29 # Example data
30 series = [10, 15, 20, 18, 22]  # Example time series data
31 alpha = 0.3
32 beta = 0.2
33 periods = 3  # Number of periods to forecast into the future
34
35 # Apply Holt's Method
36 smoothed_series, forecast = holt_method(series, alpha, beta,
    periods)
37
38 # Plotting
39 plt.figure(figsize=(10, 6))
40
41 # Plot original data
42 plt.plot(range(1, len(series) + 1), series, marker='o', color
    ='blue', linestyle='-', label='Original Data')
43
44 # Plot smoothed series
45 plt.plot(range(1, len(series) + 1), smoothed_series[:len(
    series)], color='green', linestyle='-', label='Smoothed
    Series')
46
```

```
47 # Plot forecasted values
48 plt.plot(range(len(series) + 1, len(series) + periods + 1),
        forecast[len(series):], marker='x',
49          linestyle='--', color='orange', label='Forecast')
50
51 # Axes labels and title
52 plt.title("Holt's Method (Double Exponential Smoothing)")
53 plt.xlabel('Period')
54 plt.ylabel('Value')
55
56 # Add legend and grid
57 plt.legend()
58 plt.grid(True)
59
60 # Show plot
61 plt.show()
```

5.11.4 Applications of Holt-Winters Coefficient

The Holt-Winters method is a popular technique for predicting time series data with seasonal trends in a variety of fields, such as supply chain management and retail demand forecasting – predicting sales for online and physical stores, forecasting energy usage, and financial forecasts based on economic factors and stock prices. By incorporating both trend and seasonal components, the Holt-Winters method provides robust forecasts that can aid decision-making and planning in diverse industries.

5.12   Forecasting

In this section, the process of forecasting future values using the Holt-Winters method is examined, illustrating how this approach can uncover patterns within historical data to make accurate predictions. This method involves initializing level, trend, and seasonal estimates, iteratively updating these estimates using smoothing equations, and then forecasting future values based on the refined estimates. By following these steps, one can gain valuable insights into future trends and make informed decisions.

5.12.1 The Art and Science of Forecasting

Consider a business owner who is continuously balancing staffing requirements, marketing plans, and inventories. Using forecasting as a guide, one can navigate the unknowns of the future. Forecasting is the skill of predicting future values of a variable, such as impending sales, using past data and external variables. Think of it as a method to anticipate future trends by leveraging historical data and patterns.

There are two primary methods for forecasting.

Quantitative Forecasting: Numbers Speak Volumes
This approach uses statistical models and historical data to produce forecasts. Imagine a mathematical sorcerer employing formulas to discern patterns and seasonal fluctuations from historical data points.

Qualitative Forecasting: The Wisdom of Experience
This approach considers expert opinions, findings from market research, and other subjective criteria to predict future events. It's akin to using the combined expertise of seasoned business professionals to guide forecasts.

5.12.2 Harnessing the Power of Predictive Analytics

Predictive analytics goes beyond forecasting by making more accurate predictions about future values. It's similar to possessing a supercharged crystal ball that not only predicts the future but also explains it. Predictive analytics uses complex algorithms and a variety of data sources to find the causes of future events.

Consider managing a retail establishment and utilizing forecasting to anticipate a spike in sales around the holidays. However, predictive analytics is able to identify the exact causes of this surge, such as heightened marketing campaigns or the introduction of well-liked new products, in addition to predicting it. You will be able to take advantage of emerging trends with more strategic decision-making thanks to this deeper understanding.

5.12.3 Forecasting in Practice

Let's put our ideas into practice with a practical example. Consider examining a clothes store's monthly sales data.

Table 5-2 tells an amazing tale! Sales exhibit a distinct seasonal trend, reaching their highest point around the end of the year as seen in Figure 5-10. Forecasting methods can estimate future sales and provide guidance for marketing and inventory management decisions by examining this trend.

5.12.4 A Toolbox of Techniques: Unveiling Advanced Forecasting Models

After learning the essentials, let's take a closer look at more sophisticated forecasting methods. Envision an arsenal of specialized instruments, each tailored to address a distinct forecasting problem. These are a few of the most widely used models.

Table 5-2. Example Dataset
1 for Studying Forecasting

Month	Sales
Jan	10000
Feb	12000
March	15000
April	11000
May	9000
June	8000
July	7000
August	8000
September	10000
October	12000
November	14000
December	16000

Figure 5-10. Monthly sales for clothing stores

Moving Average: Smoothing Out the Wrinkles

This methodology uses an average of a predetermined number of historical data points to smooth out data volatility. Consider it as smoothing out the kinks in your sales data to uncover hidden patterns, especially useful for addressing seasonal fluctuations.

Exponential Smoothing: Prioritizing the Latest Trends

By giving more weight to more recent data points, this model gives priority to the newest patterns. Consider it as assigning greater weight to the most recent sales data to reflect the most recent peaks and valleys in your company.

Regression Analysis: Building a Formula for Success
This method develops a mathematical relationship between one or more influencing elements and a crucial metric. To comprehend how adjustments to these components affect your outcomes, it's similar to creating a formula.

ARIMA (Autoregressive Integrated Moving Average)
This robust approach excels at managing complicated data that has seasonality, trends, and random fluctuations. It is a flexible solution for a range of forecasting difficulties since it builds a full forecasting model using historical data points and their temporal differences.

Choosing the appropriate model for the task at hand is crucial to good forecasting. Similar to selecting the ideal tool for a remodeling project, you must take your data's properties and your individual objectives into account.

5.13   Stationarity

This chapter analyzes the notion of stationarity, looks at its several manifestations, shows how to find stationarity, and describes how to convert non-stationary time series into stationary ones. Since many effective time series forecasting and modeling techniques rely on the assumption that the underlying data is stationary, an understanding of stationarity is essential.

A stationary time series exhibits statistical properties that remain consistent over time. A time series can be considered stationary if it fulfills the following criteria:

Constant mean: Over time, there are no discernible regular upward or downward trends or changes in the time series' average value.

Constant variance: Over the course of the observation period, the time series' variability around its mean stays largely constant.

Constant autocorrelation structure: Over various time intervals, the autocorrelation function (ACF), which calculates the correlation between a time series and its historical values (lags), remains constant.

5.13.1 Types of Stationarity

Characteristics such as the mean, variance, and autocorrelation structure do not change as time progresses. Hence, it's important to distinguish between two primary types of stationarity.

Strict Stationarity
When the joint probability distribution of all sets of observations is independent of the time of observation, a time series is said to be strictly stationary. This definition of stationarity is more exacting.

Weak Stationarity (Also Known As Covariance Stationarity)

A time series meets the three previously mentioned requirements (constant mean, variance, and autocorrelation structure) to be considered weakly stationary. In actuality, most time series analysis methods often make good use of weak stationarity.

Detecting Stationarity

A crucial assumption of many time series models is stationarity. These models are intended to find trends and connections in past data, then extrapolate those trends into the future to come up with predictions. Several tools and techniques can be employed to assess whether a time series is stationary.

Visual Inspection

By plotting the time series, one can get information about possible trends, seasonality, and variance variations. A stationary time series has a tendency to oscillate with a somewhat constant amplitude of variations around a constant mean.

Augmented Dickey-Fuller (ADF)

To find stationarity, one of the most popular techniques is to use this statistical hypothesis test. The time series' non-stationarity is the null hypothesis for the ADF test.

KPSS Test

The Kwiatkowski–Phillips–Schmidt–Shin test works with the opposite null hypothesis – it assumes that the time series is stationary.

5.13.2 Transforming Non-stationary Data

If the statistical properties of the underlying data change over time, the effectiveness of these models is compromised, as their forecasts may become unreliable. Hence, it is necessary to transform non-stationary data. If a time series is detected as non-stationary, the following transformations can often help to render it stationary.

Differencing

Calculating the difference between successive observations in a time series is known as differencing. Through capturing the shift between data points instead of the absolute numbers themselves, this approach seeks to eliminate seasonality and trends. The number of times this differencing must be applied is indicated by the sequence of differencing.

Log Transformation

Each data point in the time series is logarithmized (either base 10 or natural logarithmically) as part of the log transformation. This method works exceptionally well for stabilizing a series' variance when working with data that shows exponential growth or decay.

Detrending

Detrending is the process of taking the time series' trend component out. This can be done in a number of ways, like by subtracting the expected trend values from the initial observations and fitting a linear regression line to the data.

5.14 Moving Average Models

This chapter will examine the idea of moving average models in the context of time series analysis and discuss the predictive uses of these models. The innate feature of time series data is the sequential ordering of observations over time. Moving average models are a useful tool for reducing the impact of brief variations in time series data and highlighting cyclical or underlying trends.

5.14.1 Simple Moving Average (SMA)

The Simple Moving Average (SMA) is the most basic type of moving average model. The average of a predetermined number of historical observations within a time series is used to compute the SMA. We refer to this quantity of observations as the "window size." A new SMA value is computed when the window advances in time. As a filter, the SMA reduces noise and facilitates the discovery of patterns in the data.

Illustrative example: Consider a stock's closing price over a period of time. Calculating a ten-day SMA would involve taking the average of the past ten closing prices for each successive day.

Practical use in predictive analytics: You can use the SMA as a basic forecasting tool. One may determine whether there is a general upward or downward trend in the data by looking at the direction of the SMA line. SMAs do, however, have a trailing effect because they only take historical data into account.

5.14.2 Weighted Moving Average (WMA)

An improvement over the SMA is a Weighted Moving Average (WMA). More recent observations in a WMA are given greater weights during computation. This resolves an issue with the SMA's equal weighting of all points inside the window. Because the WMA prioritizes recent data, it is marginally more sensitive to shifts in the time series' underlying trend. Let's understand this weighting mechanism:

Linear weighting: In a WMA, linear weight assignment is the most popular method. The most recent data point in a linear WMA is given the largest weight, and the weights of earlier observations inside the window decrease linearly as they go older.

Example calculation: Suppose you want to calculate a five-day WMA. The weights might be assigned as follows:

Day 5 (most recent): 5/15 Day 4: 4/15 Day 3: 3/15 Day 2: 2/15 Day 1: 1/15
Notice how the weights add up to 1. The WMA is then calculated by multiplying
each data point by its respective weight and summing the results.

5.14.3 Exponential Moving Average (EMA)

A more advanced kind of moving average model is the Exponential Moving Average
(EMA). With exponentially decreasing weights applied to previous observations,
EMAs prioritize recent data. Compared to SMAs or WMAs, they are thought to
be more responsive to the most recent information. EMAs are frequently used to
determine trend directions and possible reversals in technical analysis of financial
data.

The smoothing factor: Alpha is a common smoothing factor used to indicate the
degree of weighting in an Exponential Moving Average (EMA). The range of
values for alpha is zero to one. More current data is given more weight when the
alpha is greater, while older data is given more weight when the alpha is lower.

Example calculation: The Exponential Moving Average (EMA) calculation is
recursive:

$$\text{EMA}_{\text{today}} = (\alpha \times \text{Price}_{\text{today}}) + ((1 - \alpha) \times \text{EMA}_{\text{yesterday}}) \qquad (5\text{-}3)$$

where

- α is the smoothing factor, typically defined as $\alpha = \frac{2}{n+1}$, where n is the number of periods.
- $\text{Price}_{\text{today}}$ is the current data point or price.
- $\text{EMA}_{\text{yesterday}}$ is the EMA calculated for the previous period.

Start with an initial SMA (Simple Moving Average) to serve as the first EMA
value. Then, apply the EMA formula recursively for each subsequent data point.

Example with Data

Consider the following data points for prices over five days:

Day	Price
1	50
2	52
3	51
4	53
5	54

Thus, the three-day EMA values for days 4 and 5 are 52 and 53, respectively.

Solution in detail

Day	Price	EMA Calculation	EMA
1	50	-	-
2	52	-	-
3	51	Initial SMA = $\frac{50+52+51}{3}$	51
4	53	$(0.5 \times 53) + (0.5 \times 51)$	52
5	54	$(0.5 \times 54) + (0.5 \times 52)$	53

Day 1 to Day 3

- **Prices:** The price data points are 50, 52, and 51.
- **EMA calculation:** There is no EMA calculation for these initial days because we first need a baseline value.
- **EMA:** The EMA is not available for these days because we are starting with an initial Simple Moving Average (SMA) for the first EMA calculation.

Day 3

- **Price:** 51
- **EMA calculation:** We calculate the initial SMA for the first three days to use as the initial EMA value:

$$\text{SMA}_{\text{initial}} = \frac{50 + 52 + 51}{3} = 51$$

- **EMA:** The EMA for Day 3 is set to this initial SMA value, which is 51.

Day 4

- **Price:** 53
- **EMA calculation:** We apply the EMA formula using the price for Day 4 and the EMA from Day 3:

$$\text{EMA}_4 = (\alpha \times \text{Price}_4) + ((1 - \alpha) \times \text{EMA}_3)$$

Substituting the values:

$$\text{EMA}_4 = (0.5 \times 53) + (0.5 \times 51) = 26.5 + 25.5 = 52$$

- **EMA:** The EMA for Day 4 is 52.

Solution in detailed(continued)

Day 5

- **Price:** 54
- **EMA calculation:** We apply the EMA formula using the price for Day 5 and the EMA from Day 4:

$$EMA_5 = (\alpha \times Price_5) + ((1 - \alpha) \times EMA_4)$$

Substituting the values:

$$EMA_5 = (0.5 \times 54) + (0.5 \times 52) = 27 + 26 = 53$$

- **EMA:** The EMA for Day 5 is 53.

5.14.4 Visualizations and Considerations

Plotting the computed averages with the original time series data is a common method of visualizing moving average models. The way the moving average reveals the underlying patterns and evens out volatility is made more evident by this juxtaposition. It is also of utmost importance to understand the key consideration points, which are

Window size: Selecting the right window size is essential. The moving average will respond to recent changes more quickly with a smaller window, but it will also be more noisy. Although a broader window produces a smoother line, it could not catch sudden changes in the trend.

Model selection: The desired degree of reactivity to recent data and the significance of smoothing out oscillations determine which of the three models – SMA, WMA, and EMA – to use.

5.15 Autoregressive Moving Average (ARMA) Model

The Autoregressive Moving Average (ARMA) model is a popular time series modeling approach that combines both autoregressive (AR) and moving average (MA) components. It is generally expressed as

$$X_t = c + \phi_1 X_{t-1} + \phi_2 X_{t-2} + \cdots + \phi_p X_{t-p} + \epsilon_t + \theta_1 \epsilon_{t-1} + \theta_2 \epsilon_{t-2} + \ldots$$
$$+ \theta_q \epsilon_{t-q} \tag{5-4}$$

where

- X_t is the time series at time t.
- c is a constant.
- $\phi_1, \phi_2, \ldots, \phi_p$ are the autoregressive parameters.
- ϵ_t is white noise with mean zero and variance σ^2.
- $\theta_1, \theta_2, \ldots, \theta_q$ are the moving average parameters.

The ARMA model is used for modeling stationary time series data where both the autocorrelation and partial autocorrelation functions decay exponentially or as a sinusoidal function. It is often estimated using methods like maximum likelihood estimation (MLE) or least squares.

5.15.1 Autoregressive Integrated Moving Average (ARIMA) Model

An Autoregressive Integrated Moving Average (ARIMA) model is a statistical analysis tool used for understanding and predicting future trends based on time series data. Key points about ARIMA include the following:

- ARIMA models use autoregressive (AR) components to forecast future values based on past values. This approach is effective for predicting stock prices or company earnings.
- By utilizing historical data, ARIMA models can estimate upcoming values.
- ARIMA employs moving average (MA) techniques to smooth out time series data, making it suitable for technical analysis and asset price forecasting.
- Autoregressive models suggest that past patterns may recur in the future, though they can be less reliable during financial crises or rapid technological changes.
- ARIMA combines three main components:
  - **Autoregression (AR):** Models where a variable regresses against its own previous values.
  - **Integration (I):** Incorporates differencing to ensure stationarity in time series data.
  - **Moving average (MA):** Uses lagged data to account for residual errors in observations.
- The notation for ARIMA is ARIMA(p,d,q), where
  - p: Number of lag observations included in the model (AR order)
  - d: Degree of differencing needed to make the series stationary
  - q: Size of the moving average window (MA order)
- ARIMA models are adjusted to remove trends or seasonal patterns from data, ensuring stationarity.
- To apply ARIMA, practitioners analyze autocorrelation and partial autocorrelation functions to determine suitable values for p, d, and q.
- While ARIMA models leverage historical data for forecasting, they do not guarantee future performance due to market unpredictability.

ARIMA models offer benefits in forecasting based on past data trends, but caution is needed as they rely on the assumption that historical patterns influence future outcomes.

Summary

This chapter provided a comprehensive introduction to time series analysis, starting with the basics of time series objects, their characteristics, and key concepts. It explored trends and seasonal variations, including methods for decomposing time series data into components like trend, seasonality, and noise. The chapter delved into smoothing techniques and autocorrelation, highlighting their significance in forecasting. It also covered popular models such as exponential smoothing, Holt-Winters, moving average (SMA, WMA, EMA), and Autoregressive Moving Average (ARMA/ARIMA). Practical applications of these models, along with stationarity considerations, were discussed to demonstrate how time series analysis is applied in real-world forecasting and predictive analytics.

5.16   Lab Experiment

Aim: To implement time series analysis using R-Studio
Description

Exploratory Data Analysis (EDA)

Before diving into modeling, it is crucial to perform Exploratory Data Analysis (EDA) to gain a comprehensive understanding of the time series data.

Model Selection

Based on the characteristics observed in the EDA phase, select an appropriate time series model. Common models include

- **ARIMA (Autoregressive Integrated Moving Average):** A common model that uses autoregression, differencing, and moving average components to detect underlying patterns in data.
- **Seasonal decomposition:** Break down the time series into seasonal, trend, and residual components and study each independently.
- **Exponential smoothing models:** Examples include single exponential smoothing (SES), double exponential smoothing (Holt's method), and triple exponential smoothing (Holt-Winters method).

Model Fitting

Use the selected model to fit the time series data. This involves estimating the model parameters (e.g., coefficients, seasonal factors) using techniques like maximum likelihood estimation (MLE) or least squares.

Model Evaluation

Evaluate the fitted model's performance using appropriate metrics, such as mean absolute error (MAE), mean squared error (MSE), root mean squared error (RMSE), or measures like AIC (Akaike Information Criterion) or BIC (Bayesian Information Criterion).

Forecasting

Once the model has been validated, use it to predict future time points. Forecasting can be performed utilizing the fitted model parameters and iterating over future time steps.

Validation

Validate the anticipated values against real data to determine the model's predictive accuracy. Techniques like cross-validation and holdout validation can be applied. **Input Data/Dataset:** The Hotel Booking Dataset is a comprehensive collection of data on hotel reservations designed to aid analysis and predictive modeling in the hospitality industry. This dataset contains a variety of variables that include booking information, client demographics, and reservation specifications across multiple hotels.

Technology Stack Used: R-Studio

```
1  library(tidyverse) # Metapackage of all tidyverse packages
2  list.files(path = "../input")
3  hotelData <- read.csv('../input/hotel-booking-demand/hotel_
       bookings.csv')
4  suppressPackageStartupMessages(library(tidyverse))
5  suppressPackageStartupMessages(library(pROC))
6  library(lubridate)
7
8  # Time series Analysis with Seasonal Component using MLR
9  # Filter Bookings which are checkout and group by month
10 hdd <- hotelData %>%
```

```
11    filter(reservation_status == 'Check-Out') %>%
12    group_by(reservation_status_date, arrival_date_month) %>%
13    summarise(n = n())
14  hdd$reservation_status_date <- as.Date(hdd$reservation_status
       _date)
15
16  hd <- hdd %>%
17    group_by(Date = floor_date(reservation_status_date, "month"
       )) %>%
18    summarise(NumberOfBookings = sum(n)) %>%
19    mutate(Month = month(Date)) %>%
20    add_column(Timeperiod = 0:26)
21
22  hd$Month <- as.factor(hd$Month)
23  hd <- hd[-27,]
24  hd <- hd[, c(1, 4, 3, 2)]
25
26  # Linear Regression Model building for TS forecast
27  # Model1
28  Qmodel1 <- glm(NumberOfBookings ~ Timeperiod + Month, data =
       hd)
29  summary(Qmodel1)
30  layout(matrix(c(1, 2, 3, 4), 2, 2))
31  plot(Qmodel1)
32
33  # Model2 : Quadratic Non Linear Regression
34  hd$Timeperiod2 <- hd$Timeperiod * hd$Timeperiod
35  Qmodel2 <- glm(NumberOfBookings ~ Timeperiod + Timeperiod2 +
       Month, data = hd)
36  summary(Qmodel2)
37  layout(matrix(c(1, 2, 3, 4), 2, 2))
38  plot(Qmodel2)
39
40  # Validation of the model with testing and training
41  library(caret)
42  install.packages("boot")
43  install.packages("carData")
44  library(boot)
45  library(carData)
46  library(car)
47  set.seed(4)
48  n <- nrow(hd)
49  shuffled <- hd[sample(n),]
50  train <- shuffled[1:round(0.85 * n),]
51  test <- shuffled[(round(0.85 * n) + 1):n,]
52  Qmodel2 <- glm(NumberOfBookings ~ Timeperiod + Timeperiod2 +
       Month, data = hd)
53
54  # Prediction
55  prediction <- predict.lm(Qmodel2, newdata = test)
56  prediction
57  test$NumberOfBookings
58
```

```
59  # Compute metrics R2, RMSE, MAE
60  R2(prediction, test$NumberOfBookings)
61  RMSE(prediction, test$NumberOfBookings)
62  MAE(prediction, test$NumberOfBookings)
63
64  # TIME SERIES ANALYSIS WITH FORECASTS MODELS
65  # Filter Hotel Data with reservation status and date
66  hdd <- hotelData %>%
67    filter(reservation_status == 'Check-Out') %>%
68    group_by(reservation_status_date, arrival_date_month) %>%
69    summarise(n = n())
70  hdd$reservation_status_date <- as.Date(hdd$reservation_status
       _date)
71
72  hd <- hdd %>%
73    group_by(Date = floor_date(reservation_status_date, "month"
       )) %>%
74    summarise(NumberOfBookings = sum(n))
75  hd <- hd[-27,]
76
77  ggplot(hd, aes(Date, NumberOfBookings)) + geom_line()
78
79  # Create TimeSeries for seasonal data
80  n <- length(hd$NumberOfBookings)
81  l <- 2
82  hs <- ts(hd$NumberOfBookings, start = c(2015, 7), end = c
       (2017, 8), frequency = 12)
83  trainhs <- ts(hd$NumberOfBookings[1:(n - l)], start = c(2015,
        7), frequency = 12)
84  tesths <- ts(hd$NumberOfBookings[(n - l + 1):n], end = c
       (2017, 8), frequency = 12)
85
86  # Test for stationary time series
87  library(tseries)
88  adf.test(hs)
89  kpss.test(hs)
90
91  # See the components of time series
92  components <- stl(hs, 'periodic')
93  plot(components)
94
95  library("forecast")
96  # Model 1 using auto.arima
97  Afit <- auto.arima(hs, trace = TRUE)
98  checkresiduals(Afit)
99  Aforecast <- forecast(Afit)
100 accuracy(Aforecast)
101 Aforecast
102 plot(forecast(auto.arima(hs)), sub = "Simple plot to forecast
       ")
103
104 # Model 2 using HoltWinters
105 Hfit <- HoltWinters(hs, beta = TRUE, gamma = TRUE)
```

```
106  Hfit$fitted
107  checkresiduals(Hfit)
108  Hforecast <- forecast(Hfit, h = 8)
109  accuracy(Hforecast)
110  Hforecast
111  plot(Hforecast)
112
113  # Validation of the models
114  accuracy(Aforecast)
115  accuracy(Hforecast)
```

Multiple Choice Questions

1. What is a time series?
   a. A set of data points indexed in time order
   b. A random sample of data points
   c. A collection of categorical variables
   d. A type of regression analysis
2. What does ACF stand for in time series analysis?
   a. Autoregressive correlation function
   b. Autocorrelation function
   c. Average correlation function
   d. Analytical correlation function
3. What is the primary use of the PACF plot?
   a. To identify the direct correlation between the current and past values
   b. To plot the seasonality in data
   c. To perform clustering analysis
   d. To smooth the data
4. Which of the following is a common method for decomposing a time series?
   a. Principal component analysis
   b. Singular value decomposition
   c. Seasonal-trend decomposition
   d. K-means clustering
5. What does the term "stationarity" refer to in time series analysis?
   a. Data points that are not correlated
   b. Data with a constant mean and variance over time
   c. Data that shows an increasing trend
   d. Data with seasonal patterns
6. Which model is commonly used for forecasting in time series analysis?
   a. Logistic regression
   b. K-nearest neighbors
   c. ARIMA (Autoregressive Integrated Moving Average)
   d. Decision trees
7. What does the "d" parameter represent in an ARIMA model?

a. The number of lag observations included in the model
b. The degree of differencing
c. The size of the moving average window
d. The number of seasonal periods

8. What is the purpose of differencing a time series?
   a. To increase the variability
   b. To remove the trend and make the series stationary
   c. To introduce seasonality
   d. To decrease the noise in the data

9. Which test is commonly used to check for stationarity in a time series?
   a. Chi-square test
   b. T-test
   c. Augmented Dickey-Fuller test
   d. Pearson correlation test

10. What is seasonality in time series data?
    a. Random fluctuations in data
    b. Long-term trends
    c. Repeated patterns or cycles in data at regular intervals
    d. Sudden spikes or drops in data

Long Answer Questions

1. Explain the concept of stationarity in time series analysis. Why is it important, and how can you test for stationarity in a given dataset? Provide examples of methods to make a time series stationary.

2. Discuss the components of time series decomposition. Describe the steps involved in decomposing a time series into trend, seasonal, and residual components, and explain the significance of each component in time series analysis.

3. Describe the ARIMA model and its components. How do the parameters p, d, and q influence the model, and what steps are involved in fitting an ARIMA model to a time series dataset?

4. Compare and contrast the autocorrelation function (ACF) and the partial autocorrelation function (PACF). How are these functions used in identifying appropriate models for time series data, and what insights do they provide?

5. Explain the concept of seasonality in time series data. How can you detect and model seasonal patterns, and what are the challenges associated with seasonal time series forecasting? Provide examples of methods used to handle seasonality.

Solution to MCQs

1. A set of data points indexed in time order
2. Autocorrelation function
3. To identify the direct correlation between the current and past values

4. Seasonal-trend decomposition
5. Data with a constant mean and variance over time
6. ARIMA (Autoregressive Integrated Moving Average)
7. The degree of differencing
8. To remove the trend and make the series stationary
9. Augmented Dickey-Fuller test
10. Repeated patterns or cycles in data at regular intervals

References

1. Mohit Sewak. *Deep Reinforcement Learning: Frontiers of Artificial Intelligence. Deep Reinforcement Learning*, 2019. Available at: https://api.semanticscholar.org/CorpusID:260425900.
2. Arun Kumar, Advitya Gemawat, Kabir Nagrecha, Yuhao Zhang, Side Li. *Cerebro: A Layered Data Platform for Scalable Deep Learning.* In *Conference on Innovative Data Systems Research*, 2021. Available at: https://api.semanticscholar.org/CorpusID:231685482.
3. Lynette Marais. *Data and decision making – from odd to artificial. SA Orthopaedic Journal*, 2022. Available at: https://api.semanticscholar.org/CorpusID:251000730.
4. Syed Attique Shah, Dursun Zafer Seker, M. Mazhar Rathore, Sufian Hameed, Sadok Ben Yahia, Dirk Draheim. *Towards Disaster Resilient Smart Cities: Can Internet of Things and Big Data Analytics Be the Game Changers? IEEE Access*, vol. 7, pp. 91885–91903, 2019. Available at: https://api.semanticscholar.org/CorpusID:198931117.
5. Jeni Stockman, Jonathan Friedman, John C. Sundberg, Emily Lark Harris, Lauren Bailey. *Predictive Analytics Using Machine Learning to Identify ART Clients at Health System Level at Greatest Risk of Treatment Interruption in Mozambique and Nigeria. JAIDS Journal of Acquired Immune Deficiency Syndromes*, vol. 90, pp. 154–160, 2022. Available at: https://api.semanticscholar.org/CorpusID:247317924.
6. Md. Feroz Hossain, Mohammad Alshahrani, Abdulmajeed Alasmari, Khaled Mashoor Hyderah, Ahmed Alshabab, Mutaz Ibrahim Hassan, Abdo Abdulrazzaq. *A predictive logistic regression model for periodontal diseases. Saudi Journal of Oral Sciences*, vol. 8, pp. 150–156, 2021. Available at: https://api.semanticscholar.org/CorpusID:245392611.
7. Patdono Suwignjo, Lisda Panjaitan, Ahmed Raecky Baihaqy, Ahmad Rusdiansyah. *Predictive Analytics to Improve Inventory Performance: A Case Study of an FMCG Company. Operations and Supply Chain Management: An International Journal*, 2023. Available at: https://api.semanticscholar.org/CorpusID:261690443.
8. Mahadevan Sriram. *Analysis of Minda Corporation Ltd: leveraging strategic financial tools and analytics. Emerald Emerging Markets Case Studies*, 2023. Available at: https://api.semanticscholar.org/CorpusID:265450118.
9. Patdono Suwignjo, Lisda Panjaitan, Ahmed Raecky Baihaqy, Ahmad Rusdiansyah. *Predictive Analytics to Improve Inventory Performance: A Case Study of an FMCG Company. Operations and Supply Chain Management: An International Journal*, 2023. Available at: https://api.semanticscholar.org/CorpusID:261690443.
10. Mahadevan Sriram. *Analysis of Minda Corporation Ltd: leveraging strategic financial tools and analytics. Emerald Emerging Markets Case Studies*, 2023. Available at: https://api.semanticscholar.org/CorpusID:265450118.
11. Sabiu Bala Muhammad and Rosli Saad. *Linear regression models for estimating true subsurface resistivity from apparent resistivity data. Journal of Earth System Science*, 2018, *127*: 1–10. Available at: https://api.semanticscholar.org/CorpusID:134212387.

© Ramchandra S Mangrulkar and Pallavi Vijay Chavan 2025
R. S. Mangrulkar and P. Vijay Chavan, *Predictive Analytics with SAS and R*,
https://doi.org/10.1007/979-8-8688-0905-7

12. Rabia Musheer Aziz, Prajwal Sharma, and Aftab Hussain. *Machine Learning Algorithms for Crime Prediction under Indian Penal Code*. Annals of Data Science, 2024, *11*: 379–410. Available at: https://api.semanticscholar.org/CorpusID:267407094.

13. Sameer K. Deshpande. *flexBART: Flexible Bayesian regression trees with categorical predictors*. In Proceedings of the Conference, 2022. Available at: https://api.semanticscholar.org/CorpusID:259212500.

14. Haley E. Yaremych, Kristopher J. Preacher, and Donald Hedeker. *Centering categorical predictors in multilevel models: Best practices and interpretation*. Psychological Methods, 2021. Available at: https://api.semanticscholar.org/CorpusID:245262590.

15. Milan Meloun, Martin Hill, Jiří Militký, Jana Vrbíková, Soňa Stanická, and Jan Škrha. *New methodology of influential point detection in regression model building for the prediction of metabolic clearance rate of glucose*. Clinical Chemistry and Laboratory Medicine (CCLM), 2004, 42:311–322. Available at: https://api.semanticscholar.org/CorpusID:45902909.

16. Laura Nenzi. *Learning Temporal Logic Formulas from Time-Series Data (Invited Talk)*. In Time, 2023. Available at: https://api.semanticscholar.org/CorpusID:263697343.

17. Binjie Hong, Zhijie Yan, Yingxi Chen, and Xiaobo-Jin. *Long Memory Gated Recurrent Unit for Time Series Classification*. Journal of Physics: Conference Series, vol. 2278, 2022. Available at: https://api.semanticscholar.org/CorpusID:249308543.

18. Haoyi Zhou, Shanghang Zhang, Jieqi Peng, Shuai Zhang, Jianxin Li, Hui Xiong, and Wan Zhang. *Informer: Beyond Efficient Transformer for Long Sequence Time-Series Forecasting*. In AAAI Conference on Artificial Intelligence, 2020. Available at: https://api.semanticscholar.org/CorpusID:229156802.

19. Hengxu Zhang, Zongshuai Jin, and Vladimir V. Terzija. *An Adaptive Decomposition Scheme for Wideband Signals of Power Systems Based on the Modified Robust Regression Smoothing and Chebyshev-II IIR Filter Bank*. IEEE Transactions on Power Delivery, vol. 34, pp. 220–230, 2019. Available at: https://api.semanticscholar.org/CorpusID:59233294.

20. Qingnan Fan, David Paul Wipf, Gang Hua, and Baoquan Chen. *Revisiting Deep Image Smoothing and Intrinsic Image Decomposition*. ArXiv, vol. abs/1701.02965, 2017. Available at: https://api.semanticscholar.org/CorpusID:14735611.

21. Volkan Demir, Metin Zontul, and Ilkay Yelmen. *Drug Sales Prediction with ACF and PACF Supported ARIMA Method*. 2020 5th International Conference on Computer Science and Engineering (UBMK), pp. 243–247, 2020.

22. Tomáš Cipra and Radek Hendrych. *Holt–Winters method for run-off triangles in claims reserving*. European Actuarial Journal, vol. 13, pp. 815–836, 2023. Available at: https://api.semanticscholar.org/CorpusID:258933286.

23. Anggun Yuliarum Qur'ani and Chandra Sari Widyaningrum. *The Non-Seasonal Holt-Winters Method for Forecasting Stock Price Returns of Companies Affected by BDS Action*. Mikailalsys Journal of Mathematics and Statistics, 2024. Available at: https://api.semanticscholar.org/CorpusID:267.

24. https://fastercapital.com/keyword/monthly-sales-figures.html.

25. https://cs.hse.ru/mirror/pubs/share/677928536.

26. Onkar Thorat, Nirali Parekh, and Ramchandra Mangrulkar. *TaxoDaCML: Taxonomy based Divide and Conquer using machine learning approach for DDoS attack classification*. International Journal of Information Management Data Insights, 2021, Vol. 1, Issue 2. https://doi.org/10.1016/j.jjimei.2021.100048.

27. Bhavuk Sharma and Ramchandra Mangrulkar. *Deep Learning Applications in Cyber Security: A Comprehensive Review, Challenges, and Prospects*. International Journal of Engineering Applied Sciences and Technology, 2019, Vol. 04, Issue 08. https://doi.org/10.33564/ijeast.2019.v04i08.023.

28. Karishni Mehta, Glen Dhingra, and Ramchandra Mangrulkar. *Enhancing Multimedia Security Using Shortest Weight First Algorithm and Symmetric Cryptography*. Journal of Applied Security Research, 2024, Vol. 19, Issue 2. https://doi.org/10.1080/19361610.2022.2157193.

29. Kanaad Deshpande, Junaid Girkar, and Ramchandra Mangrulkar. *Security Enhancement and Analysis of Images Using a Novel Sudoku-based Encryption Algorithm.* *Journal of Information and Telecommunication*, 2023, Vol. 7, Issue 3. https://doi.org/10.1080/24751839.2023.2183802.

30. Onkar Thorat and Ramchandra Mangrulkar. *Combining DNA Sequences and Chaotic Maps to Improve Robustness of RGB Image Encryption.* *International Journal of Computational Science and Engineering*, 2023, Vol. 26, Issue 2. https://doi.org/10.1504/IJCSE.2023.129736.

31. Sheel Sanghvi and Ramchandra Mangrulkar. *BITSAT: An Efficient Approach to Modern Image Cryptography.* *International Journal of Computational Science and Engineering*, 2023, Vol. 26, Issue 3. https://doi.org/10.1504/ijcse.2023.131501.

32. Nirali Parekh and Ramchandra Mangrulkar. *Enabling Blockchain Architecture for Health Information Exchanges.* *Unleashing the Potentials of Blockchain Technology for Healthcare Industries*, 2023. https://doi.org/10.1016/B978-0-323-99481-1.00011-0.

33. Mangesh M. Ghonge, Sabyasachi Pramanik, Ramchandra Mangrulkar, and Dac Nhuong Le. *Cyber Security and Digital Forensics.* *Cyber Security and Digital Forensics*, 2021. https://doi.org/10.1002/9781119795667.

34. Carmen López-Martín. *Dynamic analysis of calendar anomalies in cryptocurrency markets: evidences of adaptive market hypothesis.* *Revista Espanola de Financiacion y Contabilidad*, 2023, Vol. 52, Issue 4. https://doi.org/10.1080/02102412.2022.2131239.

35. Jerry L. Miller and Maynard L. Erickson. *On dummy variable regression analysis: A Description and Illustration of the Method.* *Sociological Methods & Research*, 1974, Vol. 2, Issue 4. https://doi.org/10.1177/004912417400200402.

36. Eric R. Ziegel and M. Hardy. *Regression with Dummy Variables.* *Technometrics*, 1994, Vol. 36, Issue 3. https://doi.org/10.2307/1269395.

37. U. M. Shaibu and J. C. Umeh and G. A. Abu and O. Abu and I. S. Egyir. *ECONOMETRIC MODELING OF THE NEXUS OF AGRICULTURAL POLICY AND FOOD SECURITY IN NIGERIA: A DUMMY VARIABLE REGRESSION APPROACH.* *African Journal of Food, Agriculture, Nutrition and Development*, 2023, Vol. 23, Issue 6. https://doi.org/10.18697/ajfand.121.22405.

38. Zheng Xin Wang and Hai Lun Zhang and Hong Hao Zheng. *Estimation of Lorenz curves based on dummy variable regression.* *Economics Letters*, 2019, Vol. 177. https://doi.org/10.1016/j.econlet.2019.01.021.

39. John Fox. *Dummy-Variable Regression.* In *Applied Regression Analysis and Generalized Linear Models*, 2008.

40. Josip Mikulić and Darko Prebežac. *Using dummy regression to explore asymmetric effects in tourist satisfaction: A cautionary note.* *Tourism Management*, 2012, Vol. 33, Issue 3. https://doi.org/10.1016/j.tourman.2011.08.005.

41. B.G. Tabachnick and L.S. Fidell. *Time-Series Analysis.* In *Using Multivariate Statistics*, 2013.

42. Anthony Ochieng and Mohd Hemed S and Mataka Mataka A and Juma Abdul and Odalo Ochieng J and Peter Okoli C. *A Comparative Analysis of Aspirin from Various Analgesic Formulations Using Titrimetry, Spectroscopic and Hyphenated Chromatographic Techniques.* *Journal of Molecular Imaging & Dynamics*, 2017, Vol. 7, Issue 2. https://doi.org/10.4172/2155-9937.1000134.

43. Armedy Ronny Hasugian and Heri Wibowo and Emiliana Tjitra. *Hubungan Trombositopenia, Parasitemia serta Mediator Pro dan Anti Inflamasi pada Infeksi Malaria, Timika 2010.* *Media Penelitian dan Pengembangan Kesehatan*, 2018, Vol. 28, Issue 3. https://doi.org/10.22435/mpk.v28i3.110.

44. Nur Canbolat and Serkan Bayram and Yaşar Samet Gökçeoğlu and Okan Tezgel and Mehmet Kapicioğlu and Ali Erşen and Kerem Bilsel and Mehmet İlke Büget. *Predictive prognostic factors in patients with proximal humeral fracture treated with reverse shoulder arthroplasty.* *Shoulder and Elbow*, 2023. https://doi.org/10.1177/17585732231185099.

45. Ling Kun Zhao and Yun Bo Zhao and Peng Cheng Yu and Peng Xia Zhang. *Metabolomics approach based on utra-performance liquid chromatography coupled to mass spectrometry with chemometrics methods for high-throughput analysis of metabolite biomarkers to explore the abnormal metabolic pathways associated with myocardial dysfunction.* *Biomedical Chromatography*, 2020, Vol. 34, Issue 8. https://doi.org/10.1002/bmc.4847.

46. Rogério Aparecido DEDIVITIS and Leandro Luongo Matos and André Vicente GUIMARÃES and Mario Augusto Ferrari DE CASTRO and Silvia Picado PETRAROLHA. *Neck recurrence in papillary thyroid carcinoma.* *Revista Colégio Brasileiro de Cirurgiões*, 2020, Vol. 47. https://doi.org/10.1590/0100-699120200030.

47. Arda Guler and Irem Turkmen and Seval Atmaca. *Cardiac biomarkers in predicting significant coronary artery disease in hypertrophic cardiomyopathy patients.* *Journal of Cardiovascular Medicine*, 2023, Vol. 24, Issue 4. https://doi.org/10.1177/17585732231185099.

Index

© Ramchandra S Mangrulkar and Pallavi Vijay Chavan 2025
R. S. Mangrulkar and P. Vijay Chavan, *Predictive Analytics with SAS and R*,
https://doi.org/10.1007/979-8-8688-0905-7